£2

THE WORLD'S
GREATEST

PSYCHICS
AND
MYSTICS

THE WORLD'S
GREATEST

PSYCHICS AND MYSTICS

BY
MARGARET
NICHOLAS

OCTOPUS BOOKS

ACKNOWLEDGEMENTS

The author wishes to thank Miss Eleanor O'Keefe, secretary of the Psychical Research Society, for her invaluable help and for access to the SPR Library; the *Psychic News* for access to their files; Miss Frances Johnson and Mrs Pat Kendle for useful material. As always in a book of this nature one must rely a great deal on previous works and gratitude is expressed to the following: Brian Inglis: *Natural and Supernatural* (Abacus) and *Science and Parascience* (Hodder and Stoughton); Milbourne Christopher: *Seers, Psychics and ESP* (Cassell); Dr E. J. Dingwall: *Very Peculiar People* (Rider and Co.); Ruth Brandon: *The Spiritualists* (Weidenfeld and Nicolson); Colin Wilson: *The Psychic Detectives* (Pan); Peter Underwood: *The Ghost Hunters* (Robert Hale); Paul Tabori: *Companions of the Unseen* (H. A. Humphrey Ltd) and *Harry Price* (Dennis Wheatley, Library of the Occult); Jean Burton: *Heyday of a Wizard* (George C. Harrap and Co. Ltd); Eileen J. Garrett: *My Life* (Rider and Co.) and *Many Voices* (G. P. Putnam's Sons); Doris Stokes: *Voices In My Ear* (Aidan Ellis); Julian Symons: *Conan Doyle* (Whizzard Press/Andre Deutsch); Ronald Pearsall: *Conan Doyle, A Biographical Solution* (Weidenfeld and Nicolson); Sir Oliver Lodge: *Past Years* (Hodder and Stoughton) and *Raymond* (Methuen and Co.); Peter Hurkos: *Psychic* (Arthur Barker Ltd); Jean-Charles de Fontbrune: *Nostradamus II, Into the 21st Century* (Hutchinson); Raymond Leonard: *The Nostradamus Inheritance* (Poplar Press); David Pitt Frances: *Nostradamus, Prophecies of Present Times* (Aquarian Press); Ruth Montgomery: *A Gift of Prophecy* (William Morrow and Co.); A. P. Sinnett: *Incidents in the Life of Madame Blavatsky* (George Redway); G. Blaseden Bluff: *Madame Blavatsky* (Rider and Co.); Anne Bancroft: *Twentieth Century Mystics and Sages* (Heinemann); J. R. Sturge Whiting: *Mystery of Versailles* (Rider and Co.); *The Trianon Adventure, A Symposium* (Museum Press); Joan Grant: *Time out of Mind* (Arthur Barker Ltd); A. J. Stewart: *Died 1513–Born 1929* (MacMillan); Rosemary Brown: *Unfinished Symphonies* (Souvenir Press); Morey Bernstein: *Bridey Murphy* (Hutchinson); John G. Fuller: *Jose Arigo, Surgeon of the Rusty Kinfe* (Hart Davis McGibbon); Ramus Branch: *Harry Edwards* (Ramus Branch); Paul Miller: *Born to Heal* (Spiritualist Press); Uri Geller: *My Story* (Robson Books); Jule Eisenbud: *Ted Serios* (Jonathan Cape); Matthew Manning: *The Strangers* (W. H. Allen); *The Link* (Colin Smythe); and contributors to *The Unexplained* (Orbis) especially Roy Stemman.

The publishers would like to thank the following for their kind permission to reproduce the pictures used in this book:
Topham Picture Library 2, 9, 16, 27, 32, 71, 85, 105, 115, 120, 150, 154, 159, 160; Keystone Press Agency 22, 133, 157; Fox Photos Ltd 2, 45

First published 1986
by Octopus Books Ltd
59 Grosvenor Street London W1
© 1986 Octopus Books Limited
ISBN 0 7064 2497 2
Printed in Great Britain by
Richard Clay (The Chaucer Press) Ltd,
Bungay, Suffolk

pictured on previous spread:
Left: Sir Arthur Conan Doyle
Top right: Harry Edwards
Bottom right: Theresa Neumann

Contents

Introduction

From earliest times man has been fascinated by people who claim to have experience of the occult and paranormal. Serious study is being carried out all over the world into experiences which cannot be explained in terms of our everyday existence. A national survey recently showed that more than 30 per cent of the adult population had gone through a psychic experience. An even higher percentage admitted they believed that certain human beings were endowed with psychic powers. Taking into account the frauds and cheats and charlatans, there remains an impressive body of men and women who have given convincing evidence of genuine paranormal powers. This book tells the story of some of the greatest psychics and mystics. They range from the earliest sage-like figures who predicted milestones in world history to ordinary twentieth-century housewives who found themselves with gifts of prophecy and healing. They include famous men who turned to spiritualism and peasants who discovered psychic gifts beyond anything they could have dreamed of. To read about them will, I hope, encourage you to probe a little further.

CHAPTER ONE

Powerful Mediums

They are the star performers of the psychic world.
Whether producing startling physical effects, or just
talking quietly to someone in the 'other world', they act as
channels between us and whoever is out there.

Daniel Dunglas Home

One night in December 1868 three gentlemen of 'unimpeachable reputation' sat together in the dark in an apartment on the upper floor of
Ashley House in London. One of them was Lord Lindsay, a notable
scientist, the second was Lord Adare, and the third his cousin, Captain
Charles Wynne. All three were silent, nervous and tense as though
waiting for something extraordinary to happen. After a few minutes
they heard the window in the next room being raised and almost
immediately saw the figure of Daniel Dunglas Home floating in the air
outside the window of the room in which they were sitting. He must
have been at least eighty feet from the ground. Lord Lindsay wrote
later: 'The moon was shining full into the room. . . . I saw Home's
feet about six inches above the window sill. He remained in this
position for a few seconds then raised the window, glided into the
room feet foremost and sat down.' And Lord Adare gave his word:
'The fact of his having gone out of one window and in at the other, I
can swear to.'

This astonishing feat of levitation, which is still the subject of controversy today, was performed by the Victorian psychic who is generally

regarded as the most famous medium of all time. Not only did he rise into the air with aplomb but he extended his height to an extent not thought humanly possible, washed his hands in red-hot coals, produced spirit hands out of the air, talked with phantoms, created vapours and psychic breezes and moved furniture all over the place without touching it.

Although in his mature years Home could levitate at will and became best known to the general public for his spectacular drifting about in the air, he also levitated without seemingly being aware of it. On one occasion when his host drew his attention to the fact that he was hovering above the cushion in his armchair, Home seemed most surprised. To the end of his life he maintained that he could only fly through the air because he was lifted up by the spirits. 'Since the first time, I have never felt fear,' he wrote in his autobiography, 'Should I, however, have fallen from the ceiling of some rooms in which I have been raised, I could not have escaped serious injury. I am generally lifted up perpendicularly; my arms frequently become rigid and are drawn above my head as if I were grasping the unseen power which slowly raises me from the floor. . . .'

He continued to levitate and hold remarkable séances for forty years without anyone being able to accuse him of trickery. With his handsome features, cool grey eyes and curling red-brown hair, Home was unlike any other medium of his day. Women swooned over him, and he was welcomed into aristocratic drawing rooms and palaces all over Europe and America. He was lionized by society hostesses, admired by kings and princes. The Empress Eugénie threw a fit of temper when she thought he did not pay her enough attention. Tsar Alexander II, Napoleon III and Queen Sophia of Holland welcomed him to their courts. Intellectuals like Alexandre Dumas, Thackeray and John Ruskin were fascinated by him.

Most of his séances were given in houses he had never entered before, in rooms he had never seen, often in broad daylight. He scorned the use of a curtained alcove or 'cabinet' demanded by most mediums of the day. He would enter a room modestly, dressed in elegant clothes that fitted his slender body like a glove so that his audience could see that he had no gadgetry to assist him, no room for concealment. He never took payment in cash but stayed as a guest in great style at some of the most splendid houses and happily accepted rare and expensive gifts.

Daniel Dunglas Home was born in Currie, a village near Edinburgh, on March 20, 1833. His father, William, an engineer, claimed to be the illegitimate son of the tenth Earl of Home, so on the paternal side the medium was connected with one of the most ancient and noble Border houses. His mother, Elizabeth, was said to have second sight. One of eight children, Daniel was a nervous, delicate child, probably already prone to the tuberculosis that was to affect his health all through his life. He was adopted at an early stage by a childless aunt who took him to live with her and her husband in the state of Connecticut in the United States.

Visions and apparitions, mostly connected with the death of friends or relatives, were part of his adolescence. His aunt was not sympathetic when loud knocks and raps shook the family breakfast table as he took his seat. Nor was she very pleased when her best furniture began to move about mysteriously. He was just seventeen when an exceptionally distressing outbreak of poltergeist and telekinetic phenomena upset her so badly that she threw him out of the house. He took refuge with friends who were prepared to be more understanding.

In the early 1850s, when a tidal flood of spiritualism was sweeping through America, Home began to give his first séances. With his grey eyes, auburn hair and pale complexion, he was such an attractive figure that he was soon being accepted — usually through the influence of wives — into the homes of wealthy farmers, prosperous merchants, doctors, editors, and liberal clergyman. His conversation was amusing, his manners charming. He became a perpetual houseguest whose expenses were paid and whose needs were fully met by his sponsors. He made it clear, however, that he could only produce phenomena when the spirits moved him.

Home levitated for the first time in August 1852, when he was nineteen. It happened at the home of a wealthy silk merchant called Ward Cheney in South Manchester, Connecticut. Among the guests was a journalist called Frank Burr, editor of the *Hartford Times*, a fascinated observer but a sceptic. Afterwards he described what happened:

'Suddenly, without any expectation on the part of the company, Home was taken up into the air. At first his feet were only about a foot from the floor, but it happened twice more and the third time he was carried to the ceiling of the apartment with which his head and hands came in gentle contact. He was gasping and trembling as he rose.'

Home usually, though not invariably, went into a trance at his séances. It was in Boston that his powers suddenly developed to full fruition and people began travelling hundreds of miles to see him. Complete figures began to materialize, spirit hands which wrote messages and voices which could be recognized. People clamoured for more phenomena of this nature but Home's delicate constitution was beginning to feel the strain, and his doctors advised him to go to England, where the climate tended to less extremes than in America.

He sailed for England in March 1855, and within a few weeks had found supporters of the highest social standing. Without them he would have been penniless. Those who assembled to watch him were not all

Daniel Dunglas Home

devoted believers; the majority were men and women of the world,
prepared to admit their profound scepticism when they first met him.
They included monarchs, dukes, duchesses, society hostesses and
scholarly men. Sir Edward Bulwer-Lytton, for instance, who was his
host both at his Park Lane mansion and at his stately home at Kneb-
worth, eventually acknowledged 'the extraordinary phenomena which
are elicited by his powers'.

Among the most famous sitters at his séances were the poets Robert
and Elizabeth Barrett Browning. Robert Browning loathed Home and
gave vent to his feelings in a satirical pen portrait called *Mr Sludge the*

Medium. Could it have been sheer jealousy? His wife, Elizabeth Barrett Browning, worshipped Home and remained his staunch ally to the end of her life. At one séance Home produced a garland of flowers from the atmosphere and laid it on the table, where a spirit hand took it up and placed it like a wreath of honour on Elizabeth's head. 'The hand was of the largest human size, white as snow and very beautiful,' she told a friend later. 'It was as near to me as this hand I write with, and I saw it distinctly . . . I was perfectly calm.'

Lionized in drawing room and royal court alike, Home continued to create extraordinary phenomena which even his worst enemies — Charles Dickens also detested him — failed to explain. His life was full of traumatic scenes as various jealous hostesses fought to keep the handsome medium to themselves. He had a triumphant progress through Europe, then suddenly in Italy, towards the end of 1857, announced dramatically that his mediumistic powers were about to leave him. He had been ill with tuberculosis, but on recovering went to recuperate at the home of an attractive Englishwoman who had separated from her husband. Though there was not the slightest hint of a sexual relationship, Home was riddled with guilt about the association and thought his spirit guides and controls had left him because he had behaved improperly. Fanny Trollope, the famous Victorian traveller who had been supporting Home over this period, demanded he leave the lady at once, and when he refused she withdrew her financial support.

Throughout the whole business in Italy Home felt that his invisible masters were trying to teach him a lesson. He was honest enough to acknowledge his own snobbery, love of finery and vanity. Remorseful, he joined the Roman Catholic Church and his confessor, Father Ravignon, became his close friend. Ravignon had secret hopes of persuading Home not to return to his activities as a medium, which the priest regarded as next door to witchcraft. But on the morning of February 11, 1857, the Emperor Napoleon III sent the Marquis de Belmont to ask whether M. Home had recovered his occult powers. Home sent back the answer 'Yes.'

No one was more delighted to see the medium return to his old form than the Empress Eugénie, who had complete belief in him. Home had predicted that his psychic power would leave him for a period of twelve months and he was right, to the very day. At the first séance he gave after his return there was almost a fight to get a seat. Home protested that the salon — at Count Alexander de Komar's house in the Tuileries — was far too crowded. He wanted only a small circle present. The Empress, quick to take offence, flew into a temper and swept out. Within less than an hour, however, the salon had been cleared and Eugénie returned to watch amazed as Home produced his repertoire of phenomena for the French audience as brilliantly as ever with spirit hands, vapours, tinkling chandeliers, moving furniture and levitation.

People usually arrived assuming that his séances would be, as most others were, conducted in near total darkness, as Brian Inglis points out in his *History of the Paranormal*. But Home's sittings were held in light good enough for his every action to be observed. Those who attended were usually sophisticated people, not easily duped. 'It was this combination — the calibre of the witnesses and the fact that they could see what was happening throughout the séances — that put Home in a different league from most mediums of the time.' Inglis felt that Home had somehow rediscovered the ancient abilities that shamans and witch doctors possessed, especially with regard to his capacity to levitate and withstand the effects of fire.

It was during a visit to Rome that Home met seventeen-year-old Sacha de Kroll, younger daughter of General Count de Kroll and a god-daughter of Tsar Nicholas. It was love at first sight. They sat next to each other at a supper party. 'Mr Home, you will be married before the year is ended,' she predicted to his amusement. She explained there was an old Russian superstition that this would happen if a man was seated, as Home was, between two sisters. Twelve days after their meeting, their engagement was announced. Four months later they were married in St Petersburg. Home's best man was French literary giant Alexandre Dumas. Tsar Alexander II gave them both his blessing and presented the bride with a magnificent diamond ring. When their son was born twelve months later, his birth was, said Home, accompanied by a number of signs and portents, including brilliant spirit lights and songs of invisible birds.

Home and his pretty little wife travelled continually, being received everywhere with flattering attention. They reached England in November 1859 after visiting France and Switzerland and séances were held at some of the grandest houses in the country, including those of the Duchess of Somerset and the Duchess of Sutherland. But Home's social status had undergone a subtle change. He no longer relied on patronage for his keep. His wife was wealthy. She was also the Tsar's god-daughter. He had, in other words, made a brilliant marriage.

The couple split their married life between Europe and Russia, where Home had made a friend of Count Alexis Tolstoy, who after watching a séance wrote, 'I would have gone a thousand leagues to see these things.' But fate demanded a cruel price from Home for his glittering success. After a pitifully few years of happiness Sacha became infected with tuberculosis and died in the South of France in February 1862. Home was overwhelmed with grief.

About this time, to make matters worse, he was coming under increasing attack by the sceptics. It seemed as though everyone had some idea as to how his phenomena were produced. Some of the most vitriolic remarks came from people who had never been present at a séance. Dickens, for instance, called Home an impostor but refused to watch him. Browning had become almost obsessed with depicting him as a slimy cheat.

To help himself get over the death of his wife, Home accepted every invitation offered. He held a series of séances with John Ruskin, returned to America for a spell, back to Europe then on to Russia, where the Tolstoys entertained him at their country home and he was the guest of the Tsar. He returned to England laden with emeralds and diamonds.

Exhausted by constant travel and Russian intensity, he laid low for a time, then there is a report of a remarkable séance at the North Hotel in Aberdeen. Among those who witnessed what happened was a General Boldero and his wife. Mrs Boldero reported 'The table quivered so violently and the plates rattled so much that General Boldero was obliged to stop eating.' A large armchair near the fireplace rushed across the room and up to the table, placing itself near one of the witnesses. Everyone thought this to be an astonishing manifestation, as Home had not been into the coffee room where they were at supper till they had all entered it together, and no thread or trickery of any kind could have moved the chair with the precision and velocity with which it left its place.

One of Home's firmest friends and supporters was Lord Adare, son of Lord Dunraven and one of those present on the night of Home's levitation at Ashley House. He was a Guardsman in his twenties when they met at the end of 1867. Adare, an honest English gentleman, recorded seventy-eight séances but at the end of his life said he was no nearer to understanding what happened than at the time of the recording.

In March 1871 Home submitted himself to a series of investigations by Sir William Crookes, an eminent Victorian scientist and psychic researcher. He began by showing how he could influence a spring balance from a distance, then went on to a dramatic demonstration of his control of fire. Crookes watched as he stirred up a pile of burning coals in a grate with his hand, then, taking up a red-hot lump, as big as an orange, he blew on it until it was white-hot, still cradling it in the palm of his hand.

Crookes both liked and trusted Home. In one celebrated experiment he tested the medium to see whether he could play an accordion through the power of psychokinesis. The accordion was placed in a copper cage and Home was allowed to rest his hand on the end farthest from the keys. The instrument soon began to play . . . and continued even when Home had removed his hand from it.

Everybody had expected Crookes to proclaim that Home was either a fraud or a failure. He was subjected to the most stringent test conditions. But Sir William wrote: 'The phenomena, I am prepared to attest, are so extraordinary and so directly oppose the most firmly rooted articles of scientific belief. . . .' In short, he went on to testify that in his opinion Home was what he claimed to be, a remarkable psychic medium. Crookes stuck to that opinion for the rest of his life, in spite of a great deal of derision being hurled at him. He went on to become the President of the British Association for the Advancement of Science.

On a visit to Russia Home met a beautiful dark-haired girl called Julie de Gloumeline, and after the experiments with Crookes he married her. After this second marriage, which made him financially independent, he decided to retire from the world gaze. His second marriage was as happy as his first, but from the age of thirty-eight until his death he only gave séances in small private circles.

Home was received into the Greek Orthodox Church and spent the last years of his life in Russia and the South of France. His old enemy, tuberculosis, caught up with him on June 21, 1886, at the age of fifty-three. He died at Auteuil and was buried in the Russian cemetery at Saint-Germain-en-Laye. A fine bronze bust of him is the first thing you see on entering the premises of the Society for Psychical Research in London.

Eileen Garrett

An attractive young Irish medium called Eileen Garrett leaped into the world headlines after a sensational séance at the National Laboratory of Psychical Research in London on October 7, 1930.

Two days before the séance took place the British airship R101 on its maiden passenger flight had crashed in flames at Beauvais, northern France, in the early hours of Sunday morning. Many passengers were killed in the horrific accident and the airship's captain, Flight Lieutenant Carmichael Irwin, also perished.

But the disaster was not uppermost in the minds of those who gathered in a small, darkened room at the National Laboratory as guests of its founder, Harry Price. Eileen Garrett herself did not know the purpose of the séance but had been prepared, as she always was, to offer herself for scientific research. Price was hoping that she would be able to contact his old adversary, Sir Arthur Conan Doyle, who had died a few months earlier. Australian journalist Ian Coster was there simply to observe.

Price felt that if anyone could reach Conan Doyle it would be Eileen Garrett. She had been a personal friend and knew of his desire to try to 'come through' after his death to prove what he had always believed in life — the reality of individual survival.

At three o'clock in the afternoon the séance started. After yawning deeply for several minutes, Mrs Garrett slipped into a deep trance. She spoke at first in the voice of her regular control, 'Uvani', an Indian, and conveyed various messages from the spirit world. But there was no sign of Conan Doyle.

All at once the medium became extremely agitated, tears rolled down her cheeks and Uvani's voice spelled out the name Irving or Irwin. Then a different voice came through, a breathless voice speaking in rapid, staccato outbursts and full of anguish: 'The whole bulk . . . too much for her engine capacity . . . engines too heavy . . . weather bad for long flight . . . fabric all waterlogged and ship's nose down . . . impossible to rise . . . cannot trim . . . almost scraped the roofs at Achy. . . .' On and on went the anguished voice, delivering highly technical information in a torrent of words almost too fast for Harry Price's secretary, a skilled shorthand writer who was sitting in to record the séance. 'Airscrews too small . . . fuel injection bad . . . gross lift computed badly . . . this exorbitant scheme of carbon and hydrogen entirely and absolutely wrong . . . never reached cruising altitude.' The voice at times almost reached hysteria. When it eventually faded away, everyone sat in a state of shock. There was no doubt in their minds that they had been listening to Captain Irwin of the dirigible R101.

Three weeks later Mrs Garrett reported that she had heard again from Irwin and from Sir Sefton Brancker, Director of Civil Aviation, who also died. They seemed above all anxious that people should know what had gone wrong. One thing was certain. Eileen Garrett did not know one end of an airship from the other. Experts at the Royal Airship Works at Cardington in Bedfordshire who later read the notes of the séance called it an 'astounding document' and admitted some of the details it included had been regarded as confidential.

Because Eileen Garrett appeared to know so much about the mechanics of dirigibles some people in England even suggested she should be arrested on a suspicion of espionage. But she was considered by all who knew her to be a woman of absolute integrity and an exceptional medium. Price chose her to contact Conan Doyle — which he said she eventually did — because 'she does not become emotional. She takes an academic interest in her powers, but has no explanation to offer concerning them.'

She has been described as the most thoroughly investigated medium of modern times. Most of her life was devoted to encouraging research into mediumship and its meaning, and she frequently offered herself as a guinea pig in new experiments, being as curious about the outcome as the researchers themselves.

Her personality and appearance surprised many people who had fixed ideas as to what a medium should look like. In her youth she was Eton cropped and elegant; later she attracted many by her vivacious and outgoing personality. She married three times and lost three sons, one at birth and two through illness, but she also had a daughter who shared her interests and carried on her work at the Parapsychology Foundation which she founded in New York in 1951.

Eileen Garrett was born in the historic town of Beauparc, County Meath (now in the Republic of Ireland) on March 17, 1893. One of the most familiar sights of her childhood was the Hill of Tara, ancient, mystic capital of Ireland. Her mother, Anne Brownell, who belonged to a stern Protestant family, had married a Catholic Basque named Vacho, and the religious strife that ensued led to tragedy. Eileen's mother drowned herself two weeks after her birth and her father committed suicide a few weeks later. She was brought up by an aunt and uncle, who had just returned to Ireland after service in India. The tragedy left its mark, however. In later years she rejected religion and often became impatient with the dogmatic pronouncements of some Spiritualists.

Like many sensitive children, Eileen had playmates who were invisible to others. She went to school in Meath before being sent to a boarding school in Merion Square, Dublin, where painful loneliness alternated with the joy of discovering Yeats, Synge and Joyce. When her uncle (who had been both kind and understanding) suddenly died she felt as though there was no one in the world she could turn to. Two weeks after his funeral she had her first major paranormal experience, and described it in her autobiography *Many Voices*. She wrote: 'One evening my dead uncle "appeared" to me in a vision, younger and more alert than I had known him; his Vandyke beard was well clipped and he stood strong and straight. He told me that in time I should leave my aunt and the farm and go to London. . . .' From that moment on she became interested in the whole question of life after death.

She went to London as her uncle had predicted, married an architect when she was little more than a schoolgirl and in the years that followed lost two of the sons she bore him in an epidemic of meningitis, the third at birth. The experience drained her spiritually. Left alone a great deal by her husband and perturbed by the new sensations she felt both waking and dreaming, she decided she must make a new, busy life for herself. She opened a tea room in Heath Street, Hampstead, which prospered and finally became a meeting place for some of the most famous literary men of the age. She came to know D. H. Lawrence well.

Eileen Garrett

With the outbreak of the First World War Eileen and her husband drifted apart and eventually divorced. She opened a hostel for wounded soldiers and on impulse married a sensitive artistic young soldier who was haunted by a premonition that he was going to be killed. Within a month he returned to the Front. Dining with friends at the Savoy Hotel in London one evening, she had a clairvoyant vision of her young husband being blown up with two or three of his comrades. As she sat at the dinner table she felt part of the action, and seemed to be enveloped in smoke and the stench of blood. Almost fainting, she begged to be excused. A few days later she was advised by the War Office that he was missing, believed killed. She never saw him again.

Her third marriage was to another wounded soldier, James William Garrett.

After the war she was introduced to Hewat McKenzie, director of the British College of Psychic Science, and under his guidance she began to discover the extent of her psychic powers. Sir Arthur Conan Doyle worked with her during the early days – 'He was a gentle soul and made a deep impression on me' — and Sir Oliver Lodge carried out a number of experiments with her. She was once invited to witness a Black Mass conducted by Aleister Crowley in a room in Fitzroy Square and came away unimpressed. 'If there was authority in Crowley's meetings with Lucifer I never knew it,' she wrote. 'I have really seen more uncanny things in the voodoo rites in Haiti.' She declined W. B. Yeats's invitation to collaborate with him in trying to contact the fairy people. Her scepticism was too strong.

She continued to work daily at the College, developing her faculties of telepathy, clairvoyance and clairaudience, but becoming principally known for her skill as a trance medium. Her two controls or inter-mediaries were 'Uvani', who claimed to have been a soldier in India centuries ago, and Abdul Latif, a twelfth-century physician from the Court of Saladin. In the early days she accepted them as helpers, but in time she began to doubt this and believed instead that they might be secondary personalities produced by her subconscious.

She worked on many poltergeist cases with McKenzie. Her role was to assume a trance state after she had entered the troubled house with the hope of contacting the cause of the disturbance. 'I often wondered if the whole matter was not a delusion until I saw for myself the breakages and, in some cases, wilful destruction. I was forced to the conclusion that these could well be some earthly beings with their own accounts to settle.' In the cool, detached way she had in dealing with the paranormal she decided that in the case of poltergeists the answer could often be found to stem from young children in the house with too much repressed nervous energy and a sense of discontentment. But often too she found 'an imprisoned ghost'. At one farmhouse where the father of two boys had taken a woman to live with him, she discovered the presence of the first wife, still hovering about, longing to tell her tale of their greed, injustice and intrigue. The boys, gentle children, were the unwitting channels of her poltergeist activity. The farmer, thoroughly frightened at what Eileen Garrett was discovering, ordered her out of the house and threw her umbrella after her. 'You've revealed a pretty kettle of fish,' chuckled Hewat McKenzie. She was called back, however, the farmer made a clean breast of his greed, settled his affairs decently and the poltergeist went away.

In 1931 the American Society for Psychical Research invited Mrs Garrett to New York. It was the start of years of important work in America. At Duke University she collaborated with Professor William McDougall and was invited to take part in the latest tests for extrasensory perception. She spent more than 500 hours submitting to tests by a famous New York psychologist, Dr Lawrence LeShan. One day he placed a square of material cut from a shirt in the palm of her hand. He did not tell her, but it belonged to a man who had vanished from a mid-Western city in the States and whose family were desperately trying to trace him. She not only gave a fairly accurate description of him but mentioned happenings only known within the family, and eventually stated that the man was now in La Jolla, California. He was located there and restored to his wife and children.

A spontaneous phenomenon of a physical kind occurred in 1931 when Mrs Garrett was lying on an operating table in hospital. Just after she succumbed to the anaesthetic the doctors and nurses around her heard a voice. The surgeon (who had been in India for some years) told her later that he recognized certain words of command in Hindustani. He knew it was not possible for his patient to utter a sound because of the way she had been prepared for the operation. He was so impressed by the experience that he made a special report for the records.

When she made her first visits to California in 1933 and 1935 Eileen Garrett was no different from any other tourist. She wanted to see the film studios. She did not realize, however, that what started as an amusing outing would end in an emotional confrontation with the great director Cecil B. De Mille.

On an exceedingly hot day she watched him direct a film with Elissa Landi in an Oriental setting. Soon she became aware of a little old lady standing by the side of De Mille and talking to him in a lively and vigorous manner. He did not seem to be aware of her presence, but just scratched his head and turned away. Eileen Garrett turned to her daughter, who was with her, and said, 'I think the heat must have affected my vision.'

A moment later she half turned to find the old lady standing behind her. 'She looked me straight in the face with the most vivid eyes. "I can't make him hear," she began. "I wish you would. Speak for me." '

'Who are you?' asked Eileen Garrett.

'I'm his mother. Few people know him . . . he's a lonely man.' The old lady then poured out a welter of motherly advice, encouragement, gentle criticism and loving words.

De Mille was not very pleased to see Mrs Garrett when she knocked on his door. He took her to be a hanger-on from a visiting party. But she caught his attention and passed on all the old lady had wanted to say to him. De Mille looked out of the window throughout. She was not even sure he was listening. But when he turned round tears were rolling down his cheeks. 'Where have you come from?' he asked. 'I loved my mother. It's true we didn't always understand each other but I had a great respect for her. I have waited for this for over twenty years.'

When she returned to her apartment it was filled with roses. The accompanying card from De Mille read: 'Do not come to California without first advising me.'

She was in the South of France when the Second World War broke out, and for a time ran a soup kitchen for children. She returned to New York when Paris fell and, demonstrating her wide range of interests, established a publishing firm which attracted authors of the calibre of Robert Graves and Aldous Huxley. She began to write prolifically, but after a break of ten years returned to psychical research full time, establishing the Parapsychology Foundation in New York which still supports important research.

Perhaps because of her lifelong tendency to bronchial trouble, she loved the South of France and set up the Foundation's regional headquarters at Saint Paul-de-Vence. Towards the end she preferred to take a back seat and listen to scientists, philosophers and psychical researchers talk about the latest advances in knowledge and techniques. But when she could be persuaded to discuss mediumship she was listened to with the greatest respect. She died at Saint Paul in 1970, hoping that one day a real understanding of the nature of psychic phenomena would be found.

Doris Stokes

Doris Stokes, unquestionably the most famous medium of the present day, communicates with 'the other side' as though she was talking to someone in the next room. Faint-hearted spirits are quite likely to be told, 'Speak up, dear, I can't hear you', and the over-anxious are politely requested to wait their turn.

It is her natural, almost familiar, earthy approach to the spirit world that makes her so extraordinary. On May 4, 1984, she was appearing before a huge audience in Stoke-on-Trent when she heard a familiar voice among the spirits trying to 'get through'. She gasped with surprise and cried out 'Oh no, Diana, that can't be you.' Later that evening she checked with the local radio and they told her that actress Diana Dors had just died after her courageous fight against cancer.

Also typical of her approach is the way she made contact with the popular comedian Tommy Cooper, who collapsed and died in the middle of a performance being shown on TV. Doris said that as it happened she saw him get up and leave his body. Shortly after she happened to spend the night at a hotel in Leicester where Cooper had stayed just before his death. She said, 'There was a massive bed in the room and I was looking at it when I heard Tommy's voice say "I needed that" and there was a peel of his unmistakable wild laughter.' During the night she got up to make herself a cup of tea. As she climbed between the sheets again she heard him chuckle and say 'Enjoy the bed.'

Though she has in recent years built up a massive following all over the world, Doris Stokes admits that when she was young she did not welcome the realization that she had an extraordinary gift. 'I really didn't want to know. I wanted to be normal and ordinary.' She looks ordinary enough, pleasant, grey-haired and homely in spite of the expensive beaded gowns she wears for her public performances. But several photographs taken of her while she is listening to her spirit voices reveal a strength and force that is quite startling. Her smile is wide and friendly but her grey eyes have obviously seen things that others have not.

Doris Stokes was born in Grantham, Lincolnshire, just across the road from Margaret Thatcher. Her father, blacksmith Sam Sutton, was a sensitive man and probably a natural psychic. She was only a child when she first realized that she too had a psychic gift.

One night there was a terrible fire in the next street to where she lived. Her parents, hearing that the blaze had started at their friend Tom's house, rushed out to see if they could help. Excited and curious, Doris was not able to sleep. She slipped a coat over her nightie and followed them. Crowds were gathered in the street. She craned her neck just in time to see a terrible burned shape being carried out of the house on a stretcher — all that was left of Tom. She stared, horrified yet fascinated, then lifting her eyes from the stretcher she saw something else that made her freeze. Tom was walking beside his body, real and solid-looking, not a hair singed.

Sam Sutton suddenly saw his daughter, clipped her smartly round the ear and sent her home to bed. She was still sobbing with fright and incomprehension when he came home. She described what she had seen and he patted her hair gently. He realized that night she was going to be different from other girls.

Though there was never a great deal of money, Doris was part of a good family and had a happy enough childhood. She thought her life would fall to pieces, though, when her father died. They had been so close and he had taught her so much. But before he died he said to her, 'All you've got to do is put out your hand and I'll be there to take hold.'

She was twenty when war broke out and she joined the WRAF. Life was fun, with plenty of boy friends, dances and different experiences. Sometimes, though, she was disturbed when she saw the young pilots walking out to their planes. She almost knew the ones that would not come back. Sometimes she would tell fortunes, but her predictions began to get too close to the truth. When a giggling group of WRAFs went to see 'the spook show' at the local Spiritualist church one night, the medium told her, 'One day you'll be doing this.'

Soon after she married a handsome young airman called John Fisher he was reported missing in action, and a medium at a local Spiritualist church confirmed that he had been killed. It was the most traumatic experience of her life. She had become pregnant in the early days of their marriage, and now had a baby son. She returned home in a state of shock, and what happened next is described in her autobiography, *Voices in My Ear*:

> The bedroom door flew open so sharply I thought it was my mother bursting in, and there stood my father. My mouth dropped open. He looked as real and solid as he did when he was alive. . . .
>
> 'Dad?' I whispered.
>
> 'I never lied to you, did I, Doll?' he asked.
>
> 'I don't think so,' I said.
>
> 'I'm not lying to you now. John is not with us and on Christmas Day you will have proof of this.' Then as I watched, he vanished.

Three days later the War Office informed her officially that John was dead, but to everyone's amazement she refused to believe it. They even began to think the shock had affected her mind as she clung to her hopes. Just as her father had predicted, news that John was, after all, still alive, though badly wounded, came through on Christmas Day.

She never trained as a medium but gradually became known in the Spiritualist church circuit, passing on messages from voices that became increasingly clear. Sometimes she earned a little money by giving private sittings. The death of her baby son when he was only five months old made her more conscious of her psychic gift. She was to lose three other children before she finally adopted her son Terry, and the sadness she experienced made her especially sensitive with regard to bereaved parents.

It is difficult to pinpoint exactly when she started to become a household name, but it was probably after her stunning success in America in 1978 when she went through a series of tests on television. Suddenly she was in demand everywhere. Her books became best-sellers, her public appearances great occasions. The waiting list for private sittings with her ran into thousands. She went on gruelling tours, and in Sydney the traditionally sceptical Aussies queued for hours just to get a ticket.

People were amazed at her down-to-earth attitude to the spirit world. It seemed to be as real to her as this one. Her utter belief in life after death communicated itself to her audience. Describing herself as being like a telephone exchange putting the spirits in touch with their loved ones, she performed as a clairaudient, hearing rather than seeing spirits. Sometimes she saw spirit children because she had a special empathy with them. She never promised to 'get through' to any particular person but would simply create a quiet, serene atmosphere and wait for things to happen.

The messages she gives are usually made up of trivial details, but the accuracy of these exchanges is usually enough to convince people that they are experiencing a paranormal event. Some people, trying to find a rational answer for what is going on, have suggested she is using extrasensory perception (ESP).

Those who attend her performance expecting a weird experience are disappointed. 'Hello, my loves' she greets those who have come to see her. She claims that she can see flickering blue lights above the heads of those she puts into contact. The longer a person has been dead, the stronger the voice. The newly dead tend to sound faint, sometimes fading away altogether. She has learned to cope with these awkward silences, though earlier in her life she was at times tempted to 'fill in'.

Doris Stokes recorded her contact with some very famous spirits in her book *A Host of Voices*. George Orwell, author of *Nineteen Eighty Four*, talked with her at some length. John Lennon and Marc Bolan, superstars of the pop world, came through, and so did the young actor Richard Beckinsale, who died from a heart attack when he was only thirty-two. He wanted her to tell his parents that he had taken up music, something he had always wanted to do on earth.

Doris Stokes

Perhaps the most poignant conversation she reported was with comedian Dick Emery. She has endured some traumatic physical illnesses in her life and was in hospital after her thirteenth operation for cancer when he came through. Trying to make her laugh, he joked that the spirit world wanted her so much they were taking her bit by bit.

Doris Stokes has always said there is no need to fear death. She has spent a lifetime trying to get that message over to as many people as possible.

Rudi Schneider

In the Austrian town of Braunau, where Adolf Hitler was born, two brothers, Willi and Rudi Schneider, made psychic history in the nineteen-twenties. Their father, Josef, was a typesetter with a local printing firm, a quiet, gentle man, respected in the community. Their mother, Elise, had given birth to twelve children, six of whom survived, all boys. Four of these boys were found to be mediumistic. Hans and Karl were only slightly so. The others became two of the most discussed mediums in the world.

Willi Schneider, a handsome youth with smooth, dark hair, began to show signs of psychic ability when he was fourteen; Rudi, five years his junior, demonstrated his powers when he was only eleven.

Their first experience of the supernatural was in their own home, a modest house in the main street of Braunau. His mother, fascinated by the current passion for spiritualism, decided to ask a few friends for supper so that they could experiment. Gathered round the parlour table, they used a planchette — a small board mounted on castors with a pencil attached, designed for taking spirit messages. They had little success until Willi strolled into the room and asked if he could try. When his hand rested on the planchette, it moved fluently. After a short time it began to move towards him before he even touched it.

Josef Schneider, in the meticulous account he kept of his son's career, said, 'The pencil began to write "Olga" in beautiful handwriting'. Willi had found his spirit guide. They were given to understand that Olga had once been Lola Montez, the tempestuous adventuress who was the King of Bavaria's mistress. When the family promised to say masses for her soul, she promised to make their name famous. Who or what was she? Some psychic observers believe a medium's control is his or her secondary personality dredged up from material deep in the unconscious, but this lady transferred her allegiance to Willi's brother at a later stage.

Whatever the explanation, from the moment she made herself known Willi Schneider became a subject of fascinating study for scientists all over Europe. His phenomena began in an unpretentious, domestic way. Olga apparently instructed the family to cover a kitchen stool with a large cloth and to place a handkerchief and a basin of water near it. Willi sat next to the stool, and within a short time strange things began to happen. The water began slopping about in the bowl quite violently, then two tiny hands materialized and a sound of clapping was heard. Objects placed near the stool appeared to move of their own accord. Throughout these activities Willi was fully conscious and seemed to enjoy the chaos going on around him.

Gradually news of what was happening in the Schneiders' parlour spread through the little town, causing great excitement. One of Herr Schneider's friends, Captain Fritz Kogelnik, was the first to realize the importance of what was going on. He was not a man naturally predisposed to believe in the occult, and was rather inclined to dismiss such affairs as 'antiquated medieval rubbish'. But his first encounter with Willi changed his whole attitude. 'Not even the slightest attempt was made by him to support the supernormal phenomena through normal means. He never fell into a trance at this stage in his life; he watched the manifestations with as much surprise and interest as anybody present.'

At a séance which Kogelnik attended in the early spring of 1919 when Willi was fourteen a tablecloth was slowly raised into the air, though no one was near it and the light was strong enough to see exactly what was going on. Willi was becoming, quite naturally, excited at being the centre of so much attention and Kogelnik suspected he might soon try to 'help' the phenomena in order to get more dramatic results. The Captain persuaded Herr Schneider to allow him to take Willi to his own house where he could see that his séances were rigidly controlled.

They did not have long to wait for dramatic effects. Willi began producing that strange substance known to mediums as ectoplasm. Kogelnik described it as being a cobweb-like material which first materialized at the shoulder, then wrapped itself round Willi's face. It seemed to disappear without trace. One day Kogelnik took a closer look. Standing barely a foot away from Willi's chair, he saw a faint, undulating, phosphorescent fog being emitted from the boy's head. It eventually settled on his hair like a cap before being withdrawn into the body through his nose.

Another time, Olga materialized and danced a tango in front of the astonished gathering. This was the first time that Willi had produced a full-form materialization. It did not happen often. 'The figure was about five feet tall covered with cobwebby veils,' Kogelnik recorded. 'I leaned back in my chair and they nearly touched me.' While this was going on Willi was in a deep trance, his head resting on Frau Kogelnik's shoulder as they sat comfortably on a sofa. At the end of the dance the phantom disappeared 'like lightning, just as she had come'. Those present found it very hard to convince anyone else of what they had seen.

Willi's phenomena began to attract international attention. Many scientists went to Braunau to investigate, among them Baron von Schrenck-Nötzing, one of the most important figures in psychical research in Europe. The Baron began systematic experiments with the boy in October 1919, and they were to continue for several years, during which time Willi left school and became apprenticed to a local dental technician. Schrenck-Nötzing eventually took him to Munich, where he became like an adopted son. He conducted 124 séances with the young medium and published his findings in 1924. Over ninety scientists, university teachers, doctors and other interested people had participated, and the results were claimed to be strongly positive.

The Baron found Willi Schneider to be soft-hearted, kind, obedient and modest, his actions more influenced by emotions than reasoning. He believed firmly in his mediumship. Willi was now producing the whole spectacular range of known phenomena, including sharp raps, cold winds, black shapes, the materialization of heads, hands and arms and the levitation of heavy objects. Sometimes, when they were particularly strong, he was frightened by them. Even while fully conscious he sometimes saw head-like formations and figures in white garments and veils similar to those observed during séances. The Baron was puzzled by them but came to the conclusion they were not caused by hallucination.

In May 1922 Dr E. J. Dingwall and Harry Price, the English psychical researchers, together visited Munich and after carefully checking the séance room for trap doors and false walls they watched Willi go into a trance. He was covered all over with luminous pins and there were luminous bracelets on his wrists so that they could see any movement he made in the dim light. When they returned to England Price was convinced that Willi was a remarkable medium.

He was, however, near the end of his career. His psychic talents were almost exhausted. When he visited London in 1924 his phenomena were disappointing and he decided from then on to concentrate on his dental studies. His mediumship became part-time. Waiting in the wings, however, was his younger brother, Rudi, who was to prove himself an equally remarkable medium.

At a séance one night Olga had insisted that she wanted Rudi to take part. The Schneider parents said they would not allow it because he was only eleven at the time and they thought he would be frightened. 'He will come,' said Olga through the entranced Willi. A few minutes later the young boy, apparently sleep-walking, appeared in the parlour and took his place at the table.

Rudi was a healthy, robust youngster more interested in cars and football than psychical research. On leaving school he became a motor mechanic and spent all his spare time with his pretty Austrian girl friend, Mitzi. But in a family so taken up with the supernatural he could not escape the fact that he was psychic. Olga shifted her allegiance as Willi Schneider's power waned and became Rudi's guide instead. He was to prove in some ways even more dramatic than his brother.

Herr Schneider, the boys' father, recorded in December 1925 that Rudi had been producing phenomena 'which few mortals ever got to see'. In his copious notebooks — in which details of every séance which took place in his home were carefully written down — he noted: 'At yesterday's sitting there were at least thirty appearances of an almost six-foot-high phantom. At one time there were two such phantoms. One of them touched a member of the circle.' Materialized hands were seen 'in profusion' and telekinetic phenomena were observed at a distance.

Schrenck-Nötzing more or less adopted Rudi, just as he had taken over Willi when he became his sponsor. The famous researcher conducted experiments with the younger brother first at home in Braunau, then in Munich. When the Baron died in 1929, Harry Price swiftly moved in to take his place, persuading Rudi to call him 'Uncle' and offering to become his mentor and guardian.

Things did not go too smoothly at first. The medium was not sure he wanted to continue working in the psychic field. He was more interested in trying to find a job in the motor industry in Munich, and did not particularly want to make the long journey to England which Price was suggesting. His employer in Germany, Karl Amereller, volunteered to go with him and he gave in.

Because of Price's well-known sense of showmanship and love of publicity, the new Schneider sensation was being talked about everywhere. On Rudi's first visit to England in the spring of 1929 he was scheduled to give a series of six séances. Price issued a £1,000 challenge to any conjurer or magician who could produce the simplest of the medium's phenomena under controlled conditions. No one offered to try.

By now everyone interested in psychical research was anxious to see this young Schneider. He would arrive for a séance in street clothes, then submit to being stripped, searched and dressed in a body-fitting black leotard over which he wore a black dressing gown with luminous stripes so that anyone in the room could see if he moved. He was checked for thermal rating, pulse rate and respiration — a startling

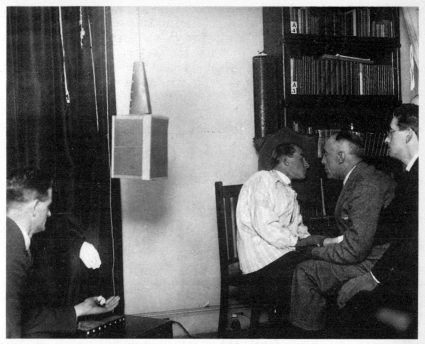

Harry Price reconstructing one of Rudi Schneider's séances

aspect of his mediumship was that his breathing was at a rate ten times or more faster than normal, yet he could keep it up for two hours at a time. He was fitted with electrical controls, and even his mouth was searched in case he had tucked away some small gadget that would help him.

The sittings in London all produced brilliant phenomena including levitation, but when he returned to Munich Frau Amereller, his employer's wife (who took a motherly interest in him), complained that Rudi had come back from England in a poor state of health. His nerves were on edge, he had little strength left and his blood pressure was much too high. He went back to work and played football for his local team before resuming séances on the Continent.

In October 1930 Rudi was invited by the distinguished Dr Eugène Osty, director of the Institut Metaphysique in Paris, to undergo a series of trials which lasted for fifteen months. With the help of his son, Marcel, the physicist had installed apparatus capable of photographing any telekinetic phenomena produced by mediums in total darkness. The photographs would give away a medium or any sitter who used physical force. Even more interesting, it was hoped that their infra-red equipment might give some clue as to *how* objects could be moved from a distance, and the identity of the force that was moving them.

The results of the trials were exciting, and impressed scientists more than anything that had gone before in the case of the Schneider brothers. The experiments pointed to the existence of a powerful force emanating from the medium which affected the infra-red rays used to test him.

There was no doubt the Osty experiments served to convince many researchers who had previously been sceptical. But once Rudi returned to Munich and took up with his old life again those closest to him began to feel his mediumship was coming to an end. His mind was not fully tuned to psychic affairs. He wanted to marry his delightful Mitzi, play football for the local team and work as a motor mechanic.

Séances trying to capture the last of his power were held at his home in Braunau under the most stringent conditions with every door and window sealed, every keyhole plastered over and with Herr Schneider locked in his bedroom. A large phantom was observed by those present, water splashed out of a basin, a handkerchief was tossed around and knotted. . . .

But blank sessions were becoming more frequent. Harry Price managed to persuade Rudi to travel to London for more experiments in which he produced faint materializations and moved objects. Photographs taken at the time show him slumped in a chair in a trance.

An automatic electric camera was used for the last séances. When the plates were being developed after the twenty-fifth session on April 28, 1932, Price saw that the camera had captured a shot of Rudi with his left arm sticking out behind his back, free from the grip of whoever should have been controlling him. Though Rudi had not produced any phenomena during that split second, Price believed that he had tried to cheat, and there was great bitterness over the incident. Others who had been present pointed out that Rudi had been startled in his trance state and could have jerked violently at the vivid photographic flash. Rudi said he could offer no explanation and remained silent about the whole business.

When Price published his report of the séance it led to such violent argument that for a time it proved a serious setback to psychical research. Many believed that Price had been jealous of the fact that Rudi Schneider had produced some of his best results under the eye of continental researchers. Strangely enough, some years later — long after the dispute had died down — Harry Price wrote, 'As far as psychical phenomena are concerned, the Schneider boys are the sheet anchor of psychical research.'

None of this mattered very much to Rudi. His powers almost gone, he married Mitzi, became a prosperous garage owner and settled in Braunau, quite happy for the rest of his life to let Olga and the phantoms sink back into the shadows from which they came.

CHAPTER TWO

Ghost Hunters

These men sought for the supernatural in many different ways, but all had dramatic experiences of powers that transcended normal human barriers.

Harry Price

The name of Harry Price, probably the most famous psychical researcher and ghost hunter England has ever known, has come to be associated in the minds of most people with his most famous case: the haunting of Borley Rectory.

Price was involved with the weird goings on at that damp, rambling Victorian mansion — the most haunted house in Britain — for nineteen years, off and on. Because his investigations, as always, had a certain flamboyance about them he was bitterly criticized by fellow researchers who did not care for his flair for publicity. But the two books he wrote about his experiences at Borley became best-sellers and opened up the whole subject of psychical research to the ordinary man in the street.

Harry Price was different from most of the serious, academic-minded men who took part in psychical research in England in the first half of this century. He had something of the showman about him, a love of drama that made him a controversial figure from his earliest days. Physically he was small in stature, stocky and bald, but he gave out a quality of vital energy and had eyes that looked right through you. Even his most bitter critics had to accept that he probably knew more about ghosts, poltergeists and haunted houses than any alive. And, showman or not, he used the latest techniques and advanced scientific methods to carry out his investigations.

His association with Borley started one day in June 1929, when he was asked by a London editor if he would investigate the strange happenings that had been reported in a local paper. For years, it seemed, anyone who took up residence at Borley Rectory – which had been built in 1863 on the site of a medieval monastery near Sudbury in Suffolk — was pestered beyond endurance by what they could only describe as supernatural forces. On his first visit Price heard enough stories to capture his scientific interest for the rest of his life. Several ghosts, it seemed, haunted the place, including a grey nun who had been seen by literally dozens of people, a headless man, a tall, dark figure and a coachman driving his carriage at full gallop. People had heard bells ringing, footsteps, wailing, knocks, bumps, rattles coming from supposedly empty rooms, crashing crockery, breaking windows, ominous dragging noises, doors opening and shutting and, from the church, the sound of music and monastic singing.

Several incumbents had been frightened away when, in 1935, the Rev. L. A. Foyster and his wife decided they too had suffered enough and announced they were leaving. Mrs Foyster, whose Christian name was Marianne, had seen messages scribbled on the wall pleading with her to get help. One day a voice called out her name and she was attacked by an invisible assailant. After hearing their story, the administrators of Queen Anne's Bounty (owners of the house) decided it was not fit for a parson to live in. They put it up for sale.

Harry Price, by now completely enthralled by the goings on at Borley, decided after some hesitation not to buy it but to offer to rent it for twelve months. As no one else wanted to set foot inside the door, his offer was accepted.

On May 19, 1937, Price, by now well known as the founder of Britain's National Laboratory for Psychical Research and the veteran of a hundred ghost watches, advertised in *The Times* for 'people of leisure and intelligence, intrepid, critical and unbiased' to join a rota of observers at the rectory. From more than two hundred people who applied, he chose forty. These stalwarts, including doctors, architects, diplomats, scientists, soldiers — a cross-section of believers and non-believers — spent some uncomfortable nights in the cold, empty rectory where one room had been set up as a base. Price's friend and neighbour of many years, Sidney H. Glanville, was in charge of operations. That Glanville was a man of utter integrity my own family can testify, for he was my father-in-law's best friend.

Many of the volunteers drew a blank. They passed some eerie, uncomfortable nights but saw or heard nothing. Others, however, had very strange experiences, ranging from seeing objects move of their own volition to hearing strange noises in empty rooms. Dr. C. E. M. Joad, the philosopher, who formed part of the team, recorded a sudden and inexplicable drop of ten degrees in the temperature of the room he slept in. Price made a formidable list of what had actually been seen and experienced.

The grey nun was seen by many, including Price, who firmly believed in her. During a séance held by some of the investigators it was discovered that the nun's name was Marie Lairre, that she had been brought to England from France by one of the Waldegraves who inhabited the original Borley Manor and that when he wanted to contract a more 'suitable' marriage he strangled her and hid her body.

Confirmation of this came in an extraordinary manner. The rectory was burned to the ground in 1939, but the phenomena continued. Price received a letter from a clergyman, the Rev. W. J. Phythian Adams, Canon of Carlisle, who suggested that now the site could be excavated. Having read Price's first book on Borley and studied the plan of the rectory, he thought he knew exactly where they should dig. In August 1943 excavations began. On the exact spot the Canon had indicated — he had never visited the place — they found part of a woman's skull with the jawbone and teeth in good condition and pendants bearing religious symbols.

Some of Harry Price's fellow researchers went wild when his books on Borley Rectory were published. His findings and reports of his investigations were torn to shreds. He was even accused of having buried the nun's bones himself to make his story better. But as Paul Tabori noted in his biography of Harry Price, that took no account of his heart condition, which would have made heavy digging to a depth of three or four feet impossible.

Price was not unconscious of the antagonism he aroused among some psychical researchers. Everything he did seemed to attract attention, and he knew his love of publicity and desire to make what he did understandable to the man in the street jarred on the 'Establishment'. But his love of the unknown and the mysterious was utterly genuine.

Price was born in London in 1881 and his schooldays were coloured by his love of magicians and conjurors. As an incredulous eight-year-old he saw 'The Great Sequah' produce two pigeons out of an empty hat, and would not be content until he knew how he had done it. His father gave him a conjuring manual for his birthday. 'From that time,' he admits in his autobiography, 'I have never missed an opportunity of ascertaining, if possible, how the wonders I have witnessed were produced.'

As a boy he spent much of his spare time wandering round street markets and fairs looking at fortune tellers, hypnotists, quack doctors and conjurors and observing their methods. When he was fifteen he

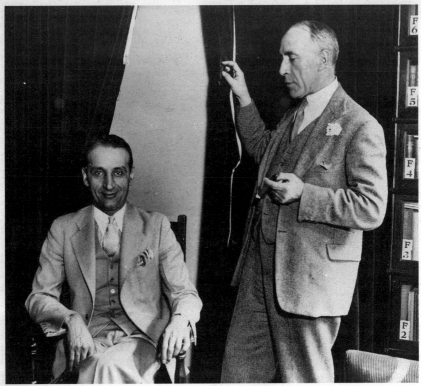

Harry Price with American medium, Frank Decker

experienced his first haunting. He used to spend many of his school
holidays in a little Shropshire village a few miles from Shrewsbury. In
the village was an old manor house which had been leased to a retired
Canon of the Church of England and his wife. Very soon after the old
couple settled there strange happenings were reported. Stable doors
would be found ajar in the morning, though fastened securely at night,
animals were discovered untethered, pans of milk overturned, logs
scattered. Servants kept watch, but saw no one. Suddenly manifestations outside ceased and terrifying activity began inside the house.
The old couple left for the sake of their health and the house was
empty when young Price talked the caretaker into letting him and his
friend spend the night there.

There was a local story that a rich recluse who had lived at the
manor many years before had strangled the young girl who kept house
for him. The old man was said to have been found drowned next day
in the river. Their restless spirits were thought to be responsible for
the disturbances. Harry Price and his friend took up their vigil in the

morning room of the manor with nothing but an old stable light to cut through the gloom and a couple of blankets to keep them warm. At about half past eleven his companion thought he heard a noise in the room above. Price heard it too, but thought it might have been rats. 'A few minutes later there was a thud overhead that left nothing to the imagination,' he wrote in his autobiography. 'It sounded as if someone had stumbled over a chair. The fact that we were not alone in the house almost paralysed us with fear.'

Just before midnight they again heard a noise in the room above, as if a heavy person was stamping about in clogs. Whatever 'it' was, it began descending the stairs. When it reached the hall, it paused before going back up again. The boys were too frightened to look out. When, about an hour after midnight, they heard footsteps on the stairs again, they decided to act. Young Price had rigged up photographic flash equipment in the hall. He pressed the switch to set it off in the room where they were hiding. There was an almighty flash and explosion and whatever was on the stairs *stumbled*. Gathering up whatever courage they had left, the boys rushed into the hall. No one was there.

The experience thrilled the young researcher and made him determined that if he ever got the opportunity he would investigate psychic phenomena on a more scientific basis. From that time on he attended every performance by a public medium he could find in the south-east of London (his home was in Brockley at this time); he went to spiritualist meetings and local séances and started to build his great library of magic and occult books.

His lively mind encompassed practical subjects as well, and he studied engineering, chemistry and photography at Goldsmiths' College in the City of London and elsewhere, and for a few years was interested in archaeology and the study of old coins. In 1908 he married a girl he had known since childhood. Though she had no interest in psychic affairs, they remained happily married for a lifetime. She had a small private income which helped to improve his financial status, and he was able to spend more time on psychical research.

During the First World War a heart ailment that troubled him all his life kept him out of active service. His knowledge of mechanical engineering, however, made him eligible to run a small munitions factory. He still found time to investigate twenty haunted houses.

By the time the war ended he had conceived a plan of great importance. He felt there should be in existence a laboratory where mediums and other psychics could be tested with the latest scientific equipment by people who had open minds on supernatural matters. He travelled all over Europe to find out what the great continental researchers were doing and in the mid-1920s opened his National Laboratory for Psychical Research in a blaze of publicity.

Price joined the Society for Psychical Research, an august body of men and women he was never really at home with, though their objects were the same: to weed out the fakes and frauds in the psychic world and concentrate on genuine phenomena. Within a very short time, he was involved in his first row. Price caused an uproar with his exposure of the revered 'spirit photographer', William Hope, whom he caught substituting a prepared plate for the marked one which had been given to him. Sir Arthur Conan Doyle, ardent spiritualist that he was, reared up in Hope's defence, and for a time his relationship with Price became very chilly indeed.

Soon after, however, Harry Price had a remarkable stroke of luck that brought him his first serious success and helped to establish his fame. In his autobiography he tells how one day he was travelling from London to his home at Pulborough in Sussex and found himself sitting opposite a young woman, a 'typical English girl with a charming personality and more than her share of good looks'. Having nothing to read on the journey she asked if she might have a look at his copy of *Light*, a psychic magazine among a pile of books and newspapers by his side. Price asked her whether she had an interest in psychic matters. She replied shyly that she had a purely objective, academic interest. Then something made her confide in him. For some years, she admitted, certain things had happened in her presence that greatly puzzled her. Perhaps two or three times a year she would find herself sitting in a perfectly quiet room with the windows closed when suddenly a strong breeze would whirl around her. Small objects moved of their own volition. There were raps and occasional flashes of light.

'Stella C.', as she was always known, turned out to be a gifted psychic who had never dreamed of becoming a medium. Harry Price persuaded her to take part in a series of séances and his detailed report on her was published internationally. She impressed some of the world's greatest scientists and researchers with her phenomena, and they believed her to be utterly genuine. Sir Julian Huxley, for instance, never forgot the curious sensations of cold he experienced in her presence. Price was impressed by her transparent honesty with regard to psychic matters, and remained grateful to her for the rest of his life.

Fake mediums had every reason to avoid him like the plague. Among those he investigated was the seventeen-stone materializing medium Helen Duncan, who produced spirit forms revealed by flashlight photographs to consist largely of cheesecloth. Observers of her in a trance state came to the conclusion that she swallowed, then regurgitated, her 'phantoms'. Price recorded that on being asked one night to agree to an X-ray examination at the National Laboratory, the large lady rushed off, opened the front door and fled screaming down the street hotly pursued by three professors, two doctors and various other sitters!

As a direct result of his report on 'Stella C.' in 1925 Harry Price was appointed as the London-based foreign research officer for the American SPR. For six years he travelled extensively, making contacts in Austria, France, Germany, Poland and Scandinavia. He worked with some of the most famous mediums of the time, probably the most famous of all being the brilliant young Austrian psychic Rudi Schneider. His association with Rudi lasted more than ten years and ended with a glorious row of the sort quite frequent in psychic circles. It blew up when Price more or less accused the Austrian boy of cheating by freeing one of his arms during a séance. There was a photograph which, he said, proved it. Everyone leaped to Schneider's defence, declaring that what had been captured by the camera could have been an involuntary trance movement. The Austrian had been regarded as one of the major discoveries of modern times, and Harry Price, accused of ulterior motives for his exposure, was out in the cold. The Schneider row rattled like a skeleton in his cupboard for years.

In 1933 he made an offer to found, equip and endow a department of psychical research at London University. Though the authorities agreed to it in principle, to his great disappointment nothing came of the idea. Late in 1936, however, he transferred to the University, on permanent loan, his magnificent collection of books on the occult and paranormal. The Harry Price Library is unique and still in constant use today. He also handed over his Laboratory. He always felt gratified that the University accepted his gifts, for it gave him a sense of public recognition. Just before the Second World War he revived the Ghost Club, which had twice faded out since it was founded in the nineteenth century. He was in his element, and at Ghost Club dinners, a dapper figure at the top table, he held its members spellbound.

His love of adventure and publicity sometimes landed him in ridiculous situations, none more so than the episode involving ancient magic on top of the Brocken in the German mountains. After it was over Professor Carl Jung, the great Swiss psychologist, wrote to him, 'For God's sake, tell me that it isn't true. How can you, a man of science, lend yourself to superstition?' His biographer, Paul Tabori, comments: 'Secretly, I think he enjoyed it all as a lark, and so did Dr Joad, his companion in this strange adventure.'

One Monday morning a person, who was never named, deposited an old manuscript entitled 'The Blocksburg Tryst', copied from the original High German 'Black Book' at the National Laboratory. Harry Price was fascinated, and announced his intention of carrying out the experiment in black magic on top of the Brocken in the Harz mountains. He arrived just in time for the Goethe centenary in 1932, accompanied by Dr Joad.

The ritual was supposed to turn a white billy goat into a handsome young man who would then be married to a 'spotless maiden'. The sight of Harry Price and Dr Joad in full evening dress on top of a

German mountain accompanied by a pretty young girl and a billy goat and bearing concoctions consisting of 'bats' blood, scraping of church bells, soot and honey' was manna for the world press, also gathered on the Brocken with cameras and notebooks.

On the ordained night the whole thing was supposed to be performed in full moonlight but there was a thick fog, and the goat remained a goat. One newspaper printed a picture of Price and Joad with the headline 'The *real* goats on the Brocken' and George Bernard Shaw laughed his head off and told Harry Price he would have liked to have been there.

The last ten years of Price's life were as full as the rest had been. He was deep into the Borley haunting, and every year answered thousands of letters from people who were interested in the occult and wanted to tell him their experiences. For years he had ignored the doctors' warnings about his heart. His work, especially at Borley, had involved long, tedious, and uncomfortable days. Haunted houses are not usually the healthiest places on earth. On Easter Monday, March 29, 1948, sitting in a chair in his study after lunch he had a major heart attack and died instantly. He was sixty-seven. Controversial to the last breath, he is still a dominating figure in psychical research.

Sir Oliver Lodge

Few books can have been received with such a storm of protest, amazement and incredulity as that which greeted the publication of *Raymond* by Sir Oliver Lodge in November 1916.

Colleagues of the distinguished physicist were appalled by its contents; friends who did not share his beliefs worried about his mental health; and the general public began to regard him as a gullible crank.

The reason? The secondary title of his famous work was 'Evidence for Survival of Memory and Affection after Death', and it consisted mainly of conversations he claimed to have had with his much-loved youngest son, Second Lieutenant Raymond Lodge, who was killed by a shell in Flanders on September 14, 1915.

Lodge was a man of immense distinction, knighted for his contribution to science and the friend of literary giants like George Bernard Shaw, but he opposed materialists and declared that his psychic experiences had led him to a profound belief in man's survival after death.

'We do not know everything that is possible to a human organism and we are certainly not aware of all existences in the universe,' he told those who accused him of chasing after ghosts. 'That my occasional psychic utterances do harm to my scientific reputation — even so far as causing some of my fellows to think me more or less cracked — is manifest,' he admitted with his usual good-humoured tolerance. 'But I feel convinced that in due time science will take investigations of this nature under its wing and will bring them into more serious consideration. . . .'

Sir Oliver Lodge was one of the founder members of the Society for Psychical Research in England. He had a great and enduring friendship with another of the great pillars of that Society, F. W. H. Myers, and often visited him at his house in Cambridge, and they would walk and talk together in the Fellows' garden at Trinity College.

Myers died in 1901, and spasmodically began to 'come through' when Lodge visited certain mediums. Myers had, after all, devoted his life to proving survival after death, and Lodge had eagerly awaited the time when his friend would clinch that proof in an unmistakable manner. But it was not until fourteen years later, when young men were being slaughtered in the trenches of the First World War, that Myers came through with a vengeance.

On August 8, 1915, a well-known American medium called Mrs Piper told Lodge that she had a message for him from Myers in the form of automatic writing. She could not understand what she had written down but there seemed to be some urgency and she advised Lodge to act as soon as possible. The message, obscure to any but a classical scholar, read 'Myers says you take the part of the poet and he will act as Faunus', adding 'Ask Verrall.'

The name Verrall referred to Mrs A. W. Verrall of Newnham College, who was one of the Cambridge nucleus of the SPR. She explained that the reference was to a passage in the *Carmen Saeculare* in which Horace thanks Faunus for protecting him from serious injury when he was felled by a tree which had been struck by lightning. In other words, Myers was telling Lodge that he must prepare himself for a great blow but that he, Myers, would do everything he could to ease the pain.

On September 14, about five weeks after the message had been received, Second Lieutenant Raymond Lodge was struck by shell fragments as he led his company back from an expedition to one of the communication trenches in Flanders. He lived for barely three hours after being wounded, and was then buried in a garden adjoining a ruined farmhouse, under some tall trees. Wooden crosses were set at the head and foot of his grave.

Grief stricken at the loss of his 26-year-old son, a handsome, young Englishman full of ebullient humour and energy, Lodge realized that his old friend Myers had been trying to warn him of his death.

Many families in England were suffering the same kind of loss as the war went on. An old friend of the Lodge family, a French lady living in London, was in great distress because she had lost both her sons within a week of each other. She asked Lady Lodge if she would accompany her to a professional medium, Mrs Osborne Leonard. Though she had never heard of Mrs Leonard at that time, Lady Lodge agreed, hoping her friend would find some comfort.

Two sittings were held, at neither of which did the ladies reveal their identity. Lady Lodge reported later that on both occasions the two sons of her French friend communicated, but with difficulty. Another personality seemed to be trying to make contact at the same time. Suddenly the medium said she had a message from someone called Raymond: 'Tell Father I've met some friends of his.' When asked if he could name any of the friends Raymond replied, 'Yes, Myers.'

Sir Oliver Lodge himself went to London two days later and without announcing who he was had his first sitting with Mrs Leonard. In a short time after the medium had gone into a trance a youth was described in terms which fitted Raymond exactly. Stumbling sentences came through . . . 'I have met hundreds of friends . . . I don't know them all . . . I feel I have got two fathers now . . . I have you both. . . .' Later sittings indicated that the second father figure was Myers, who sent Lodge the message 'Your son shall be mine.' Lodge began to see that Myers had indeed kept his word and had lightened the blow by looking after and helping his son 'on the other side'.

Other mediums were also providing messages from Raymond, including a male Dutch clairvoyant called A. Vout Peters, who told Lady Lodge that before he died her son had posed with a group of officers for a photograph. In it he was sitting down on the front row, holding a walking stick. The Lodges had never been told of the existence of such a photograph, and being naturally very anxious to see it, made many inquiries to no avail. Two months later, however, the mother of a fellow officer wrote to say she had been sent a group photograph which included Raymond and would they like to see it?

Before the photograph arrived Lodge himself went for a sitting with Mrs Leonard and in his book described how he asked Raymond, through the medium, to tell him more about it. The information that came through was that Raymond was sitting on the ground while others were standing and sitting behind him. Somebody, he remembered, insisted on leaning on his shoulder, which did not please him. When the photograph arrived there was Raymond sitting on the ground exactly as he described with a fellow officer using him as a leaning post. His son, Lodge noticed, appeared rather annoyed!

As time went on the Lodge family found the accumulation of proof that their son still existed somewhere quite 'overwhelming'. But, as Brian Inglis points out in his *History of the Paranormal*, if Lodge had been unpopular with the predominantly materialistic science establishment before, he was now out in the cold. It also made him unpopular with the Church of England, which felt threatened by Spiritualism.

Sir Oliver Lodge was one of the first of the leading members of the SPR to come right out and say that the evidence for survival had totally convinced him. Scientists made it clear that in spite of his magnificent research into such things as wireless telegraphy, he had let the side down with his ghost hunting.

But Lodge had always had a natural feeling for what he called 'the imponderables', and as a physicist was drawn to things like electricity and magnetism — 'the things that worked secretly and had to be apprehended mentally'.

He was the eldest of seven sons born into a huge, prosperous Victorian family and grew up in the Potteries, where his father made a handsome living selling raw materials to the potters of the Five Towns. He married his childhood sweetheart, Mary Marshall, a student at the Slade School of Art, and himself proceeded to build a solid, happy family life with twelve children.

From an early age he felt he was a born physicist. In the eighties and nineties of the last century he held the Professorship of Physics at Liverpool University, where he carried out some of the most important experiments of his scientific life. His research into radiation and the relation between matter and ether was highly regarded and recognized as a brilliant achievement. Thousands read his books and attended his lectures. Most people felt he thoroughly deserved the knighthood that was conferred on him on the coronation of King Edward VII.

He was on the verge of fifty when he moved from Liverpool to Birmingham to become Principal of Birmingham University. He admitted that having so large a family was no joke, and that he had to work very hard to maintain his twelve children. But he knew how to enjoy himself, too, and led a 'full, hearty Edwardian life'. When he retired from Birmingham University in 1919 and moved to the south of England, he was held in such high regard by the citizens of Edgbaston that they collected enough money to present him with a motor car, together with 'a jewel for my wife'. He was quite overcome by the feeling shown towards him. 'The kindness of everyone was very great,' he wrote afterwards.

Threaded through his success as a scientist was his increasing fascination with psychic matters. As a young man, Lodge admitted, he considered ghost stories and the like a futile occupation for a cultivated man — baseless superstition. Then in the mid-1870s he met a young Cambridge classical scholar, Edmund Gurney, who was preparing a book called *Phantasms of the Living*. Lodge was impressed by his serious approach to the subject and became even more interested when Gurney introduced him to Frederick Myers, who was collaborating with him on psychic studies.

Lodge and Myers got on famously from the start. When Gurney, Myers and others formed the Society for Psychical Research in 1882 under the presidency of the formidable Professor Henry Sidgwick, Lodge soon became a regular attender at the early meetings.

He became involved in various experiments in thought transference or telepathy and felt convinced that this explained the appearance of phantasms of the living, cases in which ghostly figures were seen by relatives of those who had been involved in traumatic accidents or who were on the point of death.

In 1889 the Professor of Psychology at Harvard University wrote to members of the SPR about the strange powers of a medium he had found in Boston called Mrs Piper. She was invited to England. Lodge met her off the boat and took her to stay with Myers, where she was judged by everybody to be a 'perfectly genuine person'.

Lodge took the opportunity of having his first sitting with a trance medium. 'Her trance was a very thorough phenomenon', he decided. 'It took her some time to get into and some time to get out of and was unmistakably genuine while it lasted.' The result was quite astonishing. 'Messages were received from all kinds of people, but the special feature was that my Aunt Anne, who had played an important part in my young life and education, ostensibly took possession of the medium . . . she spoke a few sentences in her own well-remembered voice.'

He decided to invite her to his house in Liverpool for further experiments. The visit was most successful. 'I got in touch with old relatives of whose early youth I knew nothing whatsoever and was told of incidents in their lives that were subsequently verified by their surviving elderly contemporaries.'

Lodge gradually became convinced not only of human survival but of the power of the dead to communicate (under certain conditions) with those left behind on earth, and vice versa. His conviction was strengthened when Myers 'came through' after his death and when Gurney too made contact and conversed with him. 'The persistence of the mind and memory and character of the deceased individual was abundantly demonstrated,' he declared.

Then came the war and the loss of his son in action. There was a special affinity between Sir Oliver and his youngest boy. Lodge recognized himself in Raymond as a child and as a young man. Both of them hated parties and patronizing adults when they were small, and preferred a quiet corner with a book. Both had the same passionate love of engineering and machinery. Both of them were vitally individual. Lodge was absolutely certain that his son had returned to him.

He led a retired though active life until his wife's death in 1929. His immensely readable autobiography was published in 1931, and by the time he himself died in 1940 he had acquired the aura of a wise old sage.

Of the psychic world which had occupied so much of his life he wrote:

The subject still bristles with difficulties . . . the evolution of knowledge takes time; it is to be carried on at first by a few pioneers in the face of opposition . . . I do not think that physics and psychics are entirely detached. I think there is a link between them. All I plead for is study.

Conan Doyle

Sir Arthur Conan Doyle, creator of Sherlock Holmes, the immortal fictional detective who triumphed over his adversaries by the application of pure, cold logic, was himself a man who believed in ghosts and fairies. The very epitome of an English patriot, a trained doctor who never lost his interest in medical science and a hearty, all-round sportsman, he was also a dedicated ghost hunter and one of the pioneers of psychical research.

Those who judged him purely from the outside saw only a bluff, genial extrovert, a hale and robust countryman who stood over six feet tall and weighed seventeen stone. His reputation as a tough professional writer on the one hand, and as an amateur cricketer good enough to bowl W. G. Grace on the other, did not prepare anyone for the fervent spiritualist he became later in life. But the mystic touch had always been there. It was in his genes.

The Doyles were of Catholic Irish stock and fey with it. Conan Doyle, however, was born not in Ireland but in Edinburgh on May 22, 1859. His father, Charles Doyle, at one time assistant to the surveyor in the Scottish Office of Works, became epileptic and alcoholic, spending much of his time in nursing homes. In his autobiography Conan Doyle draws a picture of him as a dreamy, aesthetic figure who, while he was never unkind to his children, did not take much notice of them either. He kept an illustrated diary which showed a distinct leaning towards the occult and an interest in fairies.

Conan Doyle was brought up in an atmosphere of genteel poverty and sent to Stonyhurst to be educated by Jesuits. Medicine was chosen for him as a 'decent' career, but while he was studying at Edinburgh he suffered great hardship through poverty. Life was no easier as the impecunious junior partner to a doctor in Sheffield, so in his twenties he signed on as a surgeon on a whaling ship. The sea toughened him both physically and mentally.

Back on land he went into practice as a GP in Southsea, a suburb of Portsmouth, and after some difficult years when he hardly had enough to live on he became established and married a quiet, gentle girl called Louise, sister of a patient he treated for meningitis. His enthusiasm and energy extended to everything. Besides his medical duties, numerous public commitments, dedication to sport and family life he had found an increasing satisfaction in writing. He had also found spiritualism.

One night in Birmingham, out of curiosity, he went to hear an American medium, J. Horstead, who seemed to be in continual contact with the Methodist preacher John Wesley — 'though occasionally Lord John Russell came through and spoke in glowing terms of Gladstone'. He started to attend Spiritualist meetings in Southsea and took part in a series of experiments which convinced him that thought transference was possible through telepathic means.

Spiritualism had reached a feverish pitch in England in the 1880s. Conan Doyle was invited to join in private séances held in the front parlours of respectable Victorian villas in Southsea and he confessed later that he enjoyed the dramatic element in many of them, especially when one night a medium called Mrs Guppy managed to materialize a huge block of ice! He was, however, still cautious.

On the formation of the Society for Psychical Research in 1882, Conan Doyle was invited to join. Though he became a member, his life was too full already for him to become deeply involved in actual research. However, he wrote in his diary that man's aim should now be to 'break down the barrier of death; to found a grand religion of the future'.

One night, after he had seen the last of his patients, he jotted down some notes on a story he proposed to write called 'A Study in Scarlet' featuring an unusual detective called Sherrinford Holmes, a name he later changed to Sherlock Holmes. The story was published and followed in quick succession by another Holmes yarn, 'The Sign of Four'. Conan Doyle became immersed in his writing, though he tended to look upon his detective stories as light relief and spent a great deal of time researching and writing books on weightier subjects, most of them now forgotten. To his amazement stories about Holmes and his friend Dr Watson, snatched from him as soon as they were written by the editor of *The Strand* magazine, created a sensation. People began to regard Holmes as a real person. They went looking for his rooms in Baker Street, begged his creator to give them more of his adventures. Conan Doyle was overjoyed. He decided to 'cut the painter' and trust in his power of writing to earn money.

There is a touch of the occult in many of his stories. He was fascinated by death, ghosts, life after death and the unknown. His great Sherlock Holmes story 'The Hound of the Baskervilles' shows him to be a master at suggesting the supernatural. He claimed he did not know what fear was, and was prepared to look any phantom straight in the eye.

He fought in the Boer War — which he regarded as a great adventure — then entered politics for a time. His private life, however, was about to become extremely complicated and overshadow everything else. For the first time in his life, he fell passionately in love.

Conan Doyle had always felt tenderly protective towards his first wife, Louise, but strong emotion had never been part of their relationship. She was ill with tuberculosis when her husband met Jean Leckie on March 15, 1897. This poised, assured woman who rode to hounds, and had trained as a singer in Dresden, aroused in him feelings he had never known before. But Conan Doyle was above all a staunch Victorian moralist and he was determined to do the 'decent thing' and stay loyal to his ailing wife. He and Jean Leckie remained lovers in name only until Louise died in 1906. They married a year later.

By 1914 Conan Doyle was part of the Establishment: knighted in 1902, famous for his books, a great champion of the Empire, a truly upstanding, conventional Englishman. The First World War brought his life to a climax but by the end of it many people began to wonder if they had ever really known him.

To start with he regarded the war as one of the greatest challenges of his life. Though he was fifty-five when it started, he flung himself into it heart and soul. His principal occupation during those four dark years was to use his genius for propaganda. He wrote stirring recruitment pamphlets, visited the Front, rallied the faint-hearted. From his home at Crowborough in Sussex he marched, drilled and organized the Southern Home Defence.

At the end of it, however, he was left like millions of others with a burden of great grief. Kingsley, the only son of his first marriage, was badly wounded at the Somme and died from pneumonia in October 1918. Only a few months later his much-loved younger brother, Innes, died too. He became determined to seek for the truth about life and death in the supernatural world.

All the wartime deaths and the suffering, far from making him bitter, convinced him that those we love must continue to exist after death. He was immensely impressed by *Raymond*, the book by Sir Oliver Lodge about his psychic contact with his dead son. Soon he started on a campaign that was to dominate the rest of his life.

Throughout the twenties Conan Doyle was totally committed to spreading the word about Spiritualism. He regarded himself as a missionary for the movement and spent a quarter of a million pounds on his lecture tours and his psychic bookshop in London. On tour he visited nearly every town in Britain, finding critical but attentive audiences everywhere.

He was intent on getting his message over to the ordinary man in the street. After a triumphant tour of this country he went to Australia and New Zealand in 1920–1 and to the United States in 1922.

He had set out his beliefs in two books produced in rapid succession just after the war. Some spiritualists were alarmed by his robust, full-blooded approach, while others rejoiced in it. Basically he saw the spirit life as being predominantly of the mind with no food, money, sex or pain but with music, the arts, intellectual and spiritual knowledge being available to all. There would be beautiful gardens, green woods, pleasant lakes and even a reunion with one's domestic pets. All religions would be treated as valid and equal. And the spirit body? He believed it would be an exact counterpart to the one we had on earth save that all disease, weakness or deformity would have disappeared. Séances, he said, had given plenty of evidence that that would be so.

At the point of death, he said, the spirit body stood or floated beside the old body, aware of it and the surroundings. The dead person could not communicate with those left behind because living organs were only tuned in to coarse stimulus. He had a clear vision of what happened next. Arriving in the hereafter, he said, the spirit body would find itself among those who had gone before. It would be welcomed then allowed to sleep for anything from a few days to several months, depending on how much trouble had been experienced in life. When the spirit had refreshed itself, it would take its place in the sphere judged most suitable — a kind of probationary limbo for the less fortunate, a clinic for the weakly souls and glorious unlimited freedom for the higher spirits, those who had fulfilled their existence on earth.

Conan Doyle seldom questioned the information passed on to him by mediums. His mother had not approved of his involvement in the psychical world and his second wife, Jean, said she too felt the subject to be 'uncanny and dangerous'. The death of her own brother, Malcolm, during the war changed her feelings. Conan Doyle described how in 1921 she suddenly acquired 'a gift of inspired writing'. From that point on the family experienced direct spirit communication. The year after Jean Conan Doyle received her 'gift' an Arabian spirit guide came through for the first time and took control so that the writing changed to inspirational talking in a semi-trance. By this means it was found possible to communicate with Malcolm Leckie, Jean's brother, and later, to Conan Doyle's joy, with his own son, Kingsley, his brother, Innes, and his brother-in-law, E. W. Hornung. The level of communication, whether by automatic writing or through the Arab guide, was always very simple. John Delane, one of the great editors of *The Times*, seems to have come through one night to tell Conan Doyle that a pleasant home was being prepared for him.

His restless search for the truth led the old warrior into some

Sir Arthur Conan Doyle, 1927

extremes from which he did not emerge unscathed. There was, for instance, the famous case of the Cottingley Fairies. Like his father before him, Conan Doyle had always been interested in the little folk of myth and legend and, perhaps because of his Irish roots, believed it possible they did exist.

In November 1920 he published an article about fairies in *The Strand* magazine along with a series of pictures of what became known as 'The Cottingley Fairies.' For weeks people talked of nothing else. Here was the creator of Sherlock Holmes solemnly giving his word that the little folk were genuine and declaring that as far as he was concerned the photographs were among the most astounding ever published. His opinions were presented against the better judgement of many experienced psychical researchers who realized that the evidence for the pictures' authenticity had not been sufficiently explored. But Conan Doyle had the bit between his teeth, and in his passion for discovering ghosts and other psychic phenomena was led up the garden path and into a fairy ring.

The culprits were two pretty young girls. One hot day in July 1917 sixteen-year-old Elsie Wright borrowed her father's camera and took a picture of her ten-year-old cousin, Frances Griffiths, playing by the river close to their home at Cottingley in Yorkshire. They gave the film to Elsie's father to develop, and he was astonished to see that the little girl in her white summer dress was surrounded by dancing fairies. The five photographs showing the tiny spectral figures caused great excitement. Was this the proof the world had been waiting for? Conan

Doyle thought so. He was responsible for introducing the Cottingley Fairies. Besides *The Strand* magazine article, which proved something of a bombshell, he was in the middle of writing a book about fairies, and used the photographs to illustrate his belief that they were real.

Just as the whole thing was beginning to get out of hand the girls confessed it had been a prank. Tired of hearing their elders and betters scoff at little Frances when, her sensitive imagination taking flight, she talked about the fairy people they had met by the river, they decided to prove what she said was true. Taking a copy of *Princess Mary's Gift Book* and some illustrations by Arthur Shepperson, they got busy with scissors and paste. Next time they went to the river they fixed them to tree trunks and the river bank, using their mothers' hatpins. What started out as a simple prank grew into an enormous deception and Conan Doyle was by no means the only eminent figure to be engulfed in its whimsy. But his critics had a field day and Bernard Partridge drew a famous cartoon in which he is shown chained by public opinion to his great fictional character, Sherlock Holmes, while his head is wreathed in the clouds of Spiritualism.

During the last decade of his life Conan Doyle travelled all over the world expounding the gospel of Spiritualism. He paid two visits to the United States, the second time taking in Canada and addressing nearly a quarter of a million people. Some thought him just an elderly crank with a bee in his bonnet. But most people were fascinated and impressed, for he could hold an audience with skill.

Always on the alert for an unusual ghost story or a spectacular tale of psychic phenomena, he went out of his way to meet an ex-gangster named Morrell, who after some time in solitary confinement in a straitjacket in an American jail found he had the ability to leave his body and stand outside it as an extra-corporeal form. He also met Marconi, who told him that he had intercepted wireless waves at a length of 30,000 metres and had speculated whether they might be messages from another planet. Conan Doyle told him he thought it more likely that they were attempts at contact from the dead.

He visited South Africa, Kenya and Rhodesia and in the late autumn of 1929 set out to take his message to Scandinavia and Holland. But his great constitution was beginning to flag. This great Victorian-Edwardian patriot did not like the modern world and felt deep depression when he realized that Spiritualism had failed to take it by storm. At the end of his Scandinavian tour he had a heart attack.

There was just one more book to write, and he worked on it during his convalescence. *The Edge of the Unknown* was a volume of essays on Spiritualistic themes. It was his farewell to a world that would remember him most of all for a character from his imagination, though to the end his adventures in the spirit world meant more to him than all his fame. He died on July 7, 1930.

Elliott O'Donnell

Doyen of ghost hunters Elliott O'Donnell once said that he thought it quite possible that some of the people we encounter and take for fellow human beings may not be of flesh and blood at all. They could be, he suggested with relish, the earthbound dead, phantasms of the living or gentle spirits drawn back to their former haunts.

It was a very Irish thing to say, but Elliott O'Donnell, who sounds as though he was a magical man to meet, was Irish to the core. His ancestry went back to Niall Niallach, legendary Irish warrior of the fourth century, sometimes styled the first O'Donnell (who was a famous ghost in his own right), and to Edgar Allan Poe, who wrote the most chilling ghost stories in the world.

Peter Underwood, President of the Ghost Club, gives a splendid account of his friend in his book *The Ghost Hunters*, and tells how he saw ghostly things, including an extraordinary nude figure covered all over with yellow spots, from the age of five.

After leaving school he applied to join the Irish Royal Constabulary, but after studying for two years failed to pass the medical exam. He had no regrets. They were, he said afterwards, among the two happiest years of his life, with plenty of time to play football and cricket, which he loved.

A tussle with a highly unpleasant ghost which tried to strangle him at his student lodgings in Waterloo Road, Dublin, was the cause of his decision to adopt ghost hunting as a profession or life work. He did not enjoy the experience, but it interested him profoundly. That interest lasted unabated for fifty ghost-ridden years.

As Peter Underwood says, it was perhaps because he was always on the lookout for adventure that he found it. But he did not look for ghosts: they came to him. At twenty years old he decided to try his luck in the New World, and in 1882 headed for America and the great open plains. Later he visited the great cities, including New York, Chicago and San Francisco. He seemed to encounter paranormal activity wherever he went.

Back in England he tried his hand at teaching, usually as a games master at various private schools. He did not find it exciting enough, and for a time joined a drama school which taught him enough to become a touring player. This too palled and he eventually settled down to teaching again after getting married.

O'Donnell and his wife decided to run a small preparatory school together in Cornwall, where he looked forward to investigating some interesting cases of haunting. He did not have to look far. A new house had been built for them close to a steep cliff, overlooking a path leading to the seashore. He moved in and prepared to open the school.

At first O'Donnell was there alone with his housekeeper, a Mrs Bolitho. Before long he began to hear strange noises at night, doors opening and shutting, footsteps ascending the stairs and walking up and down the passage outside his room. Not wishing to alarm the housekeeper he said nothing, but very soon she gave in her notice, saying she could no longer live in a house that was haunted. She thought the cause of the trouble was a set of antlers O'Donnell had inherited and hung on the wall.

Other housekeepers arrived and left and when the school opened several assistant masters complained about noises in the night. At last O'Donnell could stand it no longer and decided to set up a ghost trap. Once or twice loud knocks had shaken his bedroom door, but when he opened it nothing was there. One night he sprinkled the passage with flour and sand alternately, and fixed a line of cotton, breast high, across it. The footsteps came again, and the bang on the door, but the cotton was unbroken and the flour and sand undisturbed. Before long he closed the school and sold the house. Local people told him that before the house was built people passing the site late at night had seen a very tall figure with a small round head suddenly rise from the ground, cross the path in front of them with a swaying motion and vanish over the cliff.

Another psychic experience that happened a few years later so impressed him that he sent a report of it to the Society for Psychical Research. This was odd in a way, says Peter Underwood, because O'Donnell rather prided himself on *not* being a scientific psychical researcher, and did not see what test tubes had to do with investigating the other world or worlds.

He was standing one morning in August on the staircase of a house where he and his family were staying in Newquay, chatting to his two sisters and their old nurse who were in the hall only a few feet away from him. Something made him look up. He saw Miss Dutton, a friend who was also staying with them, come downstairs from the first landing. As she approached O'Donnell moved to one side to allow her to pass. He distinctly felt the swish of her dress against his trouser leg. She went down the hall, passed his sisters and the nurse and went into the front sitting room, slamming the door behind her.

Thinking it strange that she did not speak to them, O'Donnell and his sisters followed her into the sitting room to see if anything was wrong. There was no one there. The only exit was the door through which they had just entered. Later that morning they met her on the beach. She told them that at the moment the four people had seen her on the staircase she was walking in town with a friend.

O'Donnell became a prolific writer on supernatural and occult subjects, crime and criminology. But he liked nothing better than to be told of a haunting he had not come across before, and to make plans to investigate. He would often spend the night alone in an empty house to make his own judgement. He would have only a candle for light and that would be extinguished when things began to happen.

One of the most spine-tingling cases he investigated was centred on the house in Somerset in which, and around which, Wilkie Collins wrote *The Woman in White*. Brockley Court was built on the site of a much older house, and several occupants declared they had seen two apparitions, one quite terrible, in the early hours of the morning. O'Donnell spent his first night there in the company of a Bristol journalist, and at 2 a.m. both men saw a pillar of light move across the room and vanish close to a window. On his second visit he took three friends, while a fourth (who had walked eight miles on a wet night in his enthusiasm) turned up at ten o'clock in the morning. This friend volunteered to position himself at the end of the corridor near the top of the stairs while the rest of the party settled down in the haunted bedroom. After two hours the silence was shattered by his piercing cries for help. He told them he had fallen asleep and dreamed that a tall figure with a terrible face had come leaping up the stairway, passed him and entered the 'haunted' room. The description fitted that of a ghost seen by the owner of the property.

The party returned to the haunted room and nothing further happened until four o'clock in the morning, when one of O'Donnell's friends was nearly scared out of his wits by an apparition with a long, swarthy, skull-like face. The others could see nothing, but O'Donnell noticed a red, rectangular light about six or seven feet from the ground that had not been there before. It began to move about and seemed to pass right through him. The atmosphere was so full of terror that O'Donnell decided enough was enough and suggested they all went home. Later he plucked up courage to visit the house again with a photographer. About two in the morning spherical lights floated round the room followed by trailing mist. The photographer took a flashlight picture which when developed showed quite clearly the face of a monk.

O'Donnell had no patience with people who scoffed at the idea of ghosts or said that no phantom would ever frighten them. He had had too much experience to accept that kind of talk. Had he ever been afraid? He freely admitted that on some occasions when he had been alone and had seen or felt that which reason and instinct had told him was something supernatural and not of this world, he had indeed been very much afraid.

He attended a meeting of the Ghost Club on May 6, 1965, and died not long afterwards.

CHAPTER THREE

Reincarnations

As far as we know most of us have only had one life,
but there are people who swear they have been here
before, not once, but many times. The use of hypnotism
in which subjects are 'regressed' until they speak as
though they were other people in other centuries has
seemingly opened new frontiers.

Joan Grant

Historical novelist Joan Grant believes that she has been on this earth
at least forty times and that her 'far memory' of past lives has provided
her with material for her books.

A striking woman, beautiful in her youth, she says that in previous
lives she has been an Italian minstrel, a French prostitute, a witch, a
Red Indian and an Egyptian ruler-priest. She claims she can remember
each one of her deaths, and the even more painful experience of being
reborn. Her most distant memories are of cave paintings, taking her
back in time thousands of years.

Joan Grant's most famous book, *Winged Pharaoh*, published in
1937, translated into fourteen languages and still in print, was written
(as were her other seven historical novels) without research. She claims
it is the story of her own past life as Sekeeta, a Pharaoh's daughter
who became a ruler-priest.

Describing her technique for recalling past existences, she says she
visualizes time as a vast wheel with herself at the centre. Gazing along
the radius in any direction, towards the rim, she picks up the distant
echo of what she once was. Sometimes the details come flooding back

in dreams, at other times through psychometry, holding something of significance in her hand.

As far as this present life is concerned she came into the world on April 12, 1907, as the daughter of wealthy parents. Her father, Jack Marshall, was a brilliant scholar who became the world's greatest expert on British mosquitoes. He was an atheist, and she approved of him. Her mother, Blanche, she thought, was a mistake.

She was conceived in the Blue Grotto at Capri and remembers the resentment she felt at finding herself trapped in the body of a baby again. She had glimpses of her other lives as a small child and told stories about who she had been before she was Joan. Nobody believed her. Holidays on the long, flat beaches of Hayling Island stirred the first latent memories. Once she knew she had chased along 'a hotter, brighter shore'. She remembered herself as a Greek boy, training to be a runner, and knew the feel of his muscles and the ache in them when he had run too hard. Her family lived in a fine Edwardian house in Primrose Hill Road, London, and in her autobiography *Time out of Mind* she admits that as a schoolgirl she longed to be a unit in a crocodile, safe and ordinary, but she had war dreams that were so vivid, so real, that the stench and smell of death made her sick. For weeks she tried to keep herself from sleeping by sitting on the cold lino at the top of the stairs and pulling hairs out one by one.

Close to her scientist father, she almost convinced herself that peering through microscopes was her vocation in life. Then the famous writer H. G. Wells came to stay. He was the first, and for a long time the only, person in whom she confided. She told him about the three-dimensional, secret part of her life and he advised her, 'Keep it to yourself, Joan, until you are strong enough to bear being laughed at by fools. But never let yourself forget it, and when you are ready, write what you know about . . . it is important that you become a writer.'

Joan led the life of a gay young thing, going to hunt balls and winning cups at golf, but there was always the other self. The sight of a group of nuns in their flapping black habits would send her mind back to some terror that had happened in the sixteenth century. She would turn her eyes away and hurry in the opposite direction.

She fell in and out of love many times. Her first engagement was broken because her fiancé's parents thought she was talking rubbish when she told them about the past lives which often as she grew older came to her in the form of vivid dreams. She met her second fiancé, Esmond, on a ski-ing holiday. They felt they had met before and became engaged within twenty-four hours. They planned to marry after he had been on a business trip to France. He spent the last night before leaving for the Continent at her home, but as she saw him walk away from her down a long corridor to his bedroom she had a presentiment that she would never see him again. She was tragically right. Just before he was due to return to England, he died in a shooting accident.

Some time after, she had a dream in which she heard a voice say quite distinctly, 'Go to Leslie.' At the time she did not know what it meant, but eventually she met and married Leslie Grant, who understood and was sympathetic towards her psychic experiences. He undertook the task of writing down her far-memory dreams from dictation, so that they were recorded from the minute she woke up.

Once in the British Museum she stood looking at some ancient sculpture — a winged figure and a winged, human-headed bull from the palace of King Sargon II of Assyria, dated 721 B.C. Gradually a scene took shape before her eyes. She was a soldier, standing at the doorway of the palace at the head of a flight of steps. From the foot of the steps stretched an avenue of crouching winged bulls with a double row of palm trees behind them. Along the avenue came a procession of soldiers returning from war, bringing their prisoners and plunder with them. In one bullock cart she saw a captured sacred golden cow adorned with a jewelled necklace. Suddenly there were great cries of 'Hathor the Mighty! Hathor the Magnificent!' and the king was brought from within the cool interior of the palace on a golden litter. She saw that his black hair and beard were elaborately curled, his limbs cluttered with jewels, his nails painted scarlet. The cruelty of the soldiers towards their captives became almost too much for her to bear, when suddenly a guide came round the corner with a conducted party and broke into her dream. Joan Grant had, it seems, several lives in Egypt, not always as a woman. At one time she was a man called Ra-ab Hotep, whose story she used in two books, *Eye of Horus* and *Lord of the Horizon*. Later she was a male contemporary of Rameses II. Several of her other incarnations were equally colourful. In the middle ages she was a witch, burnt at the stake for heresy; in the sixteenth century she became a singer with a group of strolling players wandering through Italy; and in England she lived the life of a wealthy Victorian girl until she broke her back in a fall from a horse.

But it was in her life as Sekeeta, the priest-ruler of First Dynasty Egypt, about 3000 B.C., that she found the most vivid identification.

In September 1936 she was staying with an old lady called Daisy Sartorius, a friend of the family, when one night she was given a turquoise blue scarab. Holding it to her forehead, she declared it was 'warm and lively' though she herself was shivering with cold. For the next hour she slipped into another existence and described what she was seeing. 'How a girl called Sekeeta was taken from the temple of Atet to undergo the ordeal of initiation, during which she must leave her body for four days and four nights, returning at the end of the fourth day to dictate to a scribe what she had experienced.' The degree of identification deepened until she heard a faraway voice calling 'Joan, Joan' and opened her eyes to find her husband leaning over her, briskly rubbing the hand from which he had removed the scarab. Night after night she returned to her old life as Sekeeta, first as a child of three playing beside a blue pool with little scarlet fishes, later as a young girl in love, then as the priest-ruler, the 'winged pharaoh'. The most astonishing thing she discovered was that in that existence Daisy Sartorius had been her mother. That, she felt, accounted for the strong love that had grown up between them.

A similar connection was also found between a previous life and her third husband, physician and psychiatrist Denys Kelsey. They met in 1958 and found they had an immediate rapport. Joan was certain they had been together before, not once but twice. When she was a young Roman matron she took him into her house as a physician, fell in love with him and when he did not respond, ordered him to cut her wrists. Later, she says, they shared a life together in eighteenth-century England as man and wife.

After their present-day marriage they worked together as a team at their home in Pangbourne, Berkshire. Joan had gained a great deal of psychiatric experience during the war. Now, with Dr Kelsey, she offered help to many people with a unique form of psychotherapy which took into account past lives. Joan believed profoundly that events in previous existences could have an effect on the present. She found she herself, for example, was unable to summon up the courage to touch a slow worm, though she knew there was no danger. In two previous incarnations, she says, she had died from snake bite.

Asked in a BBC interview which period she would choose if she was given the option, she said immediately it would be the First Dynasty of ancient Egypt. And why? 'I think that the ethics of that benign civilization gave everyone a better chance of being happy than he is likely to be given today.'

A. J. Stewart

Ever since she was a child Ada F. Kay, successful playwright and BBC scriptwriter, had been haunted by the feeling that she was somebody else. Eerie shifts of consciousness, glimpses in the mirror of another face, scenes that receded into another century before her eyes, tormented and bewitched her, brought her near to breakdown and convinced her she had lived once before.

Who that person was she had only fleeting intimations. But one night in August 1967, while staying at a house in Jedburgh, the ancient town on the borders of England and Scotland, she learned what she believed was the truth. Her other self was James IV, the Scottish king who was killed at the Battle of Flodden in 1513 when the English forces massacred the Scots.

That night in Jedburgh she had hardly shut her eyes when with an almost audible click of consciousness she found herself on what seemed to be a sixteenth-century battlefield. Just a few yards away was a cluster of horsemen she knew to be English. One was mounted on a white charger, bearing a battle standard. There was an explosion in her head. Next minute:

I seemed to be lying on my back staring up at a tunnel of staves and blades . . . beyond them hands and merciless faces of men intent on killing me. My left arm I raised to cover my head to ward off the blows. All the world of hate was concentrated on me at that moment, and nobody was stopping it. I howled a howl of pure animal terror as the blades thrust down upon me.

The howls she let out brought her host running from another room to find his guest alone but deeply shocked.

She told him everything about her childhood experiences, her strange, passionate love for Scotland and her gradual realization as she researched material for a play about James IV that he might be her other self.

Next day he took her to Flodden, only a few miles from Jedburgh, and she almost fainted as she stood on the hillock where James's blood had been spilled. Suddenly, she was sure. The traumatic experiences the night before and at Flodden convinced her that she had been James IV in a previous life.

Ada F. Kay had what she called 'an antique memory' from earliest childhood. She was born on March 5, 1929, at Tottington in Lancashire. Her father, Ernest Kay, was a schoolmaster with a special interest in history. One of her first recollections was of seeing herself as a young prince being hauled by the hand through many stone-floored chambers and then stood on a chair to be presented by the king to his lords in council. Later she saw herself as a boy of fifteen clad in scarlet with a gold shoulder chain and riding out through a gateway at the head of a small band of horsemen while the guard rang out a salute with pike butts on cobbles. Her parents did not understand the fantastic stories she tried to tell them.

The family moved to Thornton Cleveleys on the Lancashire coast in January 1932 and Ada's antique memories went with her. She always felt she was Scottish and had a great desire to return to the North. One day waiting for a train with her parents on a station platform she saw a poster with a picture of Stirling Castle. She felt sick with excitement, forgot the new doll she had been given and tried to wish herself inside the castle gates and into another world.

During her early teens she was comparatively free from what she wryly calls 'back head interference', for her energy was being channelled into what she had a great talent for — writing. Certain things brought tingling memories. The sight of hawks or falcons reminded her of wide blue skies and open fells, and the appearance of her mother in a striking black and white evening dress brought a pang of nostalgia — were they not her royal colours?

When she was eighteen instead of going to university she opted to join the ATS and found herself stationed at Queen's Camp, Guildford. There was a strong Scottish contingent there with which she identified completely. She felt their separateness, their foreign quality and when they trooped off back to Scotland singing, 'We're no awa' tae bide awa' she felt like going with them. Only a short time later, to her delight, she was posted to Edinburgh.

As the train crossed the Tweed and the border she felt herself jolted out of a deep sleep by the thought 'I am back in Scotland.' The first time she saw Edinburgh in mist and morning rain she laughed with joy. She had been waiting eighteen years for this.

She loved the Army and her posting seemed like a gift from the gods. Only three weeks after she had arrived her parents travelled from England to see her and she was persuaded into taking them to see some of the historic sights. Much against her will, she escorted them to Edinburgh Castle along with hundreds of other tourists. Suddenly she found herself crammed into the tower room which contained Scotland's royal regalia. Her link with the crown on its velvet cushion seemed to be so intensely personal and strong that she had to look away. She gazed instead at the royal sword until she saw it trickling with blood. Hoping frantically she would not fall, she pulled herself together and the red colour cleared from her eyes. Her mother's words 'Are you all right, Ada?' seemed to come from a great distance.

Her health began to deteriorate soon afterwards and she suffered deep depressions. She continually had glimpses of Edinburgh as it was in the sixteenth century; her boundary on the north side of Edinburgh was Princes Street, beyond that she knew it was a superb place to hunt wildfowl, a marshland alive with bittern and glinting with small lochs. She took walks through the narrow alleyways of old Edinburgh searching for her past. 'I was not seeking ghosts but my own reality,' she wrote in her autobiography. One evening, from the Lawnmarket, she saw an open door, a stone spiral stair dimly lit by the pool of light cast by a gas lamp on a wall bracket. She felt she was expected, that people were waiting to greet her for supper, her host appeared, bowed low in salute and started to lead her up the stairs — then it all disappeared. Next day she tried to find the house again. But it had vanished.

Her ghosts were beginning to intrude on her Army life. From her window she could see ships in the Forth heading for Rosyth Naval Dockyard, but they were huge, black-timbered sailing ships and she knew they belonged to another age. These fleeting impressions and haunting experiences became too much for her. She asked to see the Army psychiatrist. Deciding that the balance of her mind was disturbed and she was heading for a breakdown, the Medical Board decided she had better go home. Her discharge from the Army, and therefore from Scotland, was a shock so great it made her physically sick.

As the train taking her back to England sped through the night she saw her reflection in the window. Her face looked older, narrower and gaunt, like her own but more masculine. It seemed to have a small circlet above it which flashed with points of sapphire blue light. She took it to be an optical illusion.

When she got home she burst into tears, went straight to bed and slept for three days and three nights. Picking up the threads of life again was not easy. But she was only twenty, red-haired and attractive. She began to write plays. She was prolific and undaunted by criticism. Soon her work was good enough to take her into the world of professional theatre. Her first real success, *Cardboard Castle*, was written within a week.

Ada F. Kay went to London in 1954 with £10 in cash and two suitcases, and set out to make herself into a first-class playwright. She was asked to join the BBC's script-writing team. Her play *The Man from Thermopylae*, which was first produced with Alec Clunes and Lionel Jeffries in the cast in 1956, was acclaimed a critical success.

She met and married Peter Stewart, an architect who was able to give her a priceless wedding present — a Scottish name. The marriage was made difficult by her frequent yearning for Scotland. They were happiest when both had plenty of work to do and Peter was at the drawing board while she was at the typewriter. He suggested they bought a house in Hampstead, hoping to give her roots in England.

In 1959, script-writing took her back to Glasgow, her first significant return since her discharge from the ATS. Suddenly realizing how little she knew of Scottish history, she had to take a crash course and in the pages of an old book discovered James IV with red hair like her own and a face strangely familiar. From then on the very name of Flodden sent a shiver down her spine.

Over the next few years she only visited England for necessary business arrangements, discussion of plays and BBC script conferences. Outwardly she was a successful woman who appeared at smart literary parties and wrote excellent plays. Inwardly she was full of doubts and fears as to who she really was. Once, coming out of the bathroom, she caught a glimpse in a mirror of a figure with red hair wearing a black and white surcoat over a suit of armour.

By 1963 she rarely left Edinburgh except to spend holidays on the Isle of Arran and hardly ever saw her parents. When she had been married for eight years she and Peter agreed on a divorce. For six of those years she had lived apart from him in Scotland.

Plays were still being demanded from her, and in January 1966 she decided to write one about James IV, hoping perhaps to lay a ghost. She felt the whole period covering the last three decades of the fifteenth century and the first decade of the sixteenth was her own, and by using it as a background she could express her feelings about Scotland's greatness.

The writing only emphasized the problem she was having in trying to disentangle James's personality from her own. She had begun to dress in a long black sweater and black tights with a gold belt round her waist. When she was given a bound copy of James IV's collected letters she seemed to be drawn even deeper into his personality. Then came the traumatic night in Jedburgh.

Preferring now to be known as A. J. Stewart, she has written a book about James which makes him come alive on the page. Though tending to have fits of depression each year when the anniversary of his death comes round, she leads a perfectly well-adjusted life, as writer Ian Wilson found when he visited her at her flat in Edinburgh in 1978.

Below natural red hair and striking features, A.J., as she likes to be known, was dressed in black, the costume plain except for a white collar and cuffs and at her throat a neat gold brooch emblazoned with a black falcon. Black shoes, black stockings . . . her flat lined with drawings and prints of James and personalities at his court.

He found her to be a forceful and engaging personality who demonstrates how like the James portraits she is.

Still, 'Of one thing I am certain,' wrote A. J. Stewart. 'Had I grown up in a culture which allowed the possibility that man has more lives than one, I should have been spared much suffering.'

Bridey Murphy

There was nothing about Mrs Virginia Tighe, a trim, smart young American housewife who lived in Pueblo, Colorado, to suggest she held a key to the past. She and her husband, Rex, were part of the bright, contemporary social scene and filled their lives with bridge parties, cocktails and club dances. Under hypnosis, however, Mrs

Tighe became someone quite different — a little girl who lived in nineteenth-century Ireland and whose name was Bridey Murphy.

The story of Bridey Murphy is one of the most celebrated in the records of regression hypnosis, a technique which, it is claimed, can sometimes take the subject so far back in time that previous lives are revealed.

It all began on the night of November 29, 1952.

Colorado businessman and amateur hypnotist Morey Bernstein had discovered that Virginia Tighe was a remarkably good subject. She had the ability to slip easily into a very deep trance. He asked if she would co-operate in an experiment in which he would take her back to infancy, then perhaps beyond. He had not attempted this before.

There was a feeling of suppressed excitement when she arrived at his home that night. He made her comfortable in a reclining position on a couch, lit a candle and turned off all the lights, with the exception of one lamp.

She drifted easily back through the years, reliving the memory of childhood scenes, until she was only one year old. Bernstein told her that her mind could go even further back to different scenes, in some other time. 'What do you see?' he asked her gently.

He leaned forward, holding his breath, as a child's voice with a soft Irish accent said: 'I scratched the paint off all my bed. Jus' painted it, 'n' made it pretty. It was a metal bed, and I scratched the paint off it. Dug my nails on every post and just ruined it. Was jus' terrible.'

'Why did you do that?'

'Don't know. I was just mad. Got an awful spanking.'

Her name, she told him, was Bridget or Bridey Murphy and she was four years old, had red hair and lived in a house in Cork . . . she had a brother called Duncan . . . and her father's name was Duncan too. . . .

Bridey Murphy's story slowly came together in a number of sessions in which 29-year-old Virginia Tighe slipped back into a life and character so different from her own. She had been born, she said, in Cork on December 20, 1798. She was the daughter of Duncan and Kathleen Murphy, both Protestants. Her father was a barrister in Cork and they lived in a white wooden house called The Meadows on the outskirts of town. She had a brother, Duncan, who was two years older than herself.

When she was fifteen she went to a day school run by a lady called Mrs Strayne. Asked what she had been taught at school, Bridey answered, 'Oh, to be a lady . . . just house things . . . and proper things.' Her brother married Mrs Strayne's daughter, Aime. In 1818 Bridey met a lawyer from Belfast called Sean Brian MacCarthy. His father was also a barrister and the families appeared pleased with the match, though she did not like him when she accepted his proposal.

'I just went with him . . . 'twas taken for granted, I think.'

There were certain difficulties from the outset. 'Brian', as she preferred to call him, was a Catholic, so after being married in Cork (to please her family) she had to go through another ceremony in Belfast, to please her husband. They made the journey north in a horse and carriage, and Bridey described the places they passed through.

She did not enjoy living in Belfast as much as in Cork, but seemed happy enough with Brian, and proud of the fact that he taught at Queen's University. They attended St Theresa's Church, where the priest was Father John Gorman, but she was not allowed to take communion or confession. Bridey shopped for provisions with a grocer named Farr, bought fruit and vegetables at Carrington's and blouses and camisoles at Caden House. She never had children, though she enjoyed visits to friends' houses and occasional trips to the sea. She was interested in Irish mythology, knew some Irish songs and was a neat dancer of Irish jigs. At the end of one sitting Mrs Tighe, not quite fully conscious, danced round the room.

Towards the end of her life she had a fall. Her death came quietly and without pain while her husband was at church one Sunday. She remembered that they had played the uillean pipes at her funeral. She also told how she watched her burial, describing the state of being after death. Somehow she was reborn in America, but could not explain how that had happened.

Morey Bernstein finished his sessions with Bridey Murphy in October 1953 and three years later published his best-selling book of the case, *The Search for Bridey Murphy*. In it his subject was given the pseudonym Ruth Simmons.

From the moment Bridey's story appeared in print there was a scramble to see who could be first to check the facts. Investigators and reporters swarmed over to Ireland, burrowing through records, talking to aged inhabitants and checking maps.

Some facts could not be checked. There was no possibility, for instance, of confirming the dates of marriages and deaths in Cork, as no records were kept there until 1864. On the negative side, no information could be unearthed about the wooden house called The Meadows, St Theresa's Church or Father Gorman. On the positive side, she gave an accurate description of the Antrim coastline and of the journey from Cork to Belfast. It was discovered that the shops she mentioned had all existed and the coins she mentioned in her shopping transactions had all belonged to that period. Bridey had said that uillean pipes had been played at her funeral, and it was indeed found to have been the custom because of their soft tone.

Despite certain discrepancies there was no doubt that Bridey's story gave a remarkably detailed account of the life of a fairly privileged member of the professional class in nineteenth-century Ireland. It was full of the sort of trivial, intimate information that is seldom recorded in books but has to be experienced.

Mrs Tighe emphatically denied that she had ever visited Ireland or had much to do with Irish people. But one interesting fact emerged after the publication of Bernstein's book. She had been born in Maddison, Wisconsin, where she lived with her mother and father until she was three years old — and both parents were part Irish. After that she was brought up in Chicago by a Norwegian uncle and his wife who claimed Irish blood somewhere in the family. Could she have stored knowledge she heard as such a small child? Even that does not seem enough to explain how she came to have been Bridey Murphy or how without any dramatic talent she could so enter her personality as to make her seem a real person.

Jane Evans

One of the most famous and most widely believed of all reincarnation claims is that concerning Cardiff housewife Jane Evans, who took part in an experiment in hypnosis only to find herself giving details of her past lives, including that as a twelfth-century Jewess in York.

Mrs Evans was taken back in time by a technique called 'regression' — in which the memory layers are peeled off like onion skins — by hypnotherapist Arnall Bloxham, and her story became one of the highlights of the recorded hypnosis sessions known as 'the Bloxham tapes'.

Millions saw her on television in a programme introduced by Magnus Magnusson in 1976. Bloxham had by then achieved 400 regressions with various subjects, but Jane Evans produced the most intensely dramatic results. Her scream of sheer terror as she met her death at the hands of the mob in an historic massacre seemed to most people to have come right from the heart.

Few details of Jane Evans' life were revealed apart from the fact that she was born in 1939, had received an ordinary high-school education, then went on to secretarial college. After her marriage she devoted her life to her family and was said at no time to have studied history in the depth that would have been needed for her to fake her regressions.

Under Arnall Bloxham's guidance she appeared to live again in six past existences. First she was a Roman matron called Livonia living in occupied Britain in the fourth century A.D. Her fate was entwined with that of the Roman legate (and later Emperor) Constantius, his wife Helena and their son Constantine, who would himself one day become Roman emperor. Livonia was married to Titus, Constantine's tutor, and they lived well until their conversion to Christianity. Under hypnosis she described her last hours as she ran through streets where Christian houses were burning until she and her husband seemed to come to a violent end. Experts on Roman Britain said that as Livonia she seemed to know facts that only Roman historians would have at their fingertips. They thought a great deal of research would have to be done by anyone inventing such a story.

In another life she was Alison, a beautiful young servant in the house of the fifteenth-century merchant prince Jacques Coeur. She described with great accuracy his great château in the Loire Valley with its magnificent courtyard and romantic architecture. She showed a detailed knowledge of the history of France and the life of the time. As far as the ordinary reader was concerned Jacques Coeur was, it had to be admitted, historically little known, but sceptics pointed out she could have got a great deal of her information from a work of fiction based on his life and used it unknowingly.

Briefly, it seemed, she was also Anna, maid of honour to the Spanish Infanta, Catherine of Aragon. She accompanied her to England in the

---

Dorothy Eady

For many years tourists visiting the ancient temple at Abydos on the banks of the Nile would see an elderly English woman who looked as if she belonged there. Her name was Dorothy Eady, but she only answered to Um-Seti, convinced that she was really an Egyptian priestess. She was born in 1903 into a wealthy South London family and, as a child, fell down a flight of stairs. Although she was believed dead she made a dramatic recovery and was nursed back to health. Dorothy never seemed the same child again, frequently asking to be 'taken home'. A few years later while visiting the Egyptian galleries of a museum, she ran wild, believing these to be her people and went on to study the ancient Egyptians. She married an Egyptian and went to Egypt to make her home. Their only child was named Seti and from then she called herself Um-Seti – mother of Seti. Her first pilgrimage to Abydos, the site of Seti I's temple and the tomb of Osiris was in 1952. Two years later she returned there to live for the rest of her life as she felt an overwhelming sense of place. In 1973 she asked the temple curators if she could be buried in the grounds of the temple when she died. She had convinced even them that her claim was far from ordinary. They gave their permission.

year 1501 for her marriage to Prince Arthur, eldest son of Henry VII. Another life saw her as Anne Tasker, a London sewing maid in Queen Anne's time at the turn of the 17th and 18th centuries. Her last incarnation before her present life was as Sister Grace, a member of an enclosed order of nuns in Des Moines, Iowa. For all these lives she showed a knowledge of contemporary events that one would not expect a twentieth-century Welsh housewife to have.

Most intriguing of all was the second life in her cycle of reincarnation — the life she supposedly entered some centuries after she had lived as the Roman, Livonia. It was featured in Jeffrey Iverson's programme about the Bloxham tapes on British television, when hypnosis took her back to twelfth-century York and the Jewish massacre that took place in 1190.

She said her name was Rebecca and she was the wife of a wealthy Jewish merchant in the city. She lived a luxurious and comfortable life until a bitter wave of anti-Semitism engulfed and destroyed everything she had known. She described being pursued with other Jewish families through the narrow, winding streets of York, hiding with her children in the crypt of a church, then being discovered and put to death. Her terror when the murderers entered the crypt was so real that listeners felt they were there at her actual moment of death.

The massacre of the Jews in York, while a known historical fact, is not an episode given at great length in popular history books, but Professor Barrie Dobson of York University, a leading expert on Jewish history, commented that Mrs Evans's story was true to what was known of the events.

On the tapes the Jewess, Rebecca, could not give the name of the church where she hid with her family but said it was outside the gates of the city, close to Coppergate and within sight and earshot of York Castle. After listening to her Professor Dobson felt sure this had to be St Mary's Church in Castlegate, though St Mary's did not, as far as he knew, have a crypt. Then in September 1975, after Jane Evans had put her chilling memories on tape but before the TV programme was relayed, workmen undertaking repairs at St Mary's made a discovery. Under the chancel they found what seemed to have been an ancient crypt, but thinking it of no importance they covered it over before it could be examined by archaeologists.

At the time she was working on the tapes with Bloxham, Jane Evans said she had been to Yorkshire but never to the city of York itself. Her knowledge of history, she said, was the same as any schoolgirl's. She enjoyed reading but had never read history books or even books of historical fiction that contained such information. She knew that Jews had been persecuted all over the world but had never heard of this particular massacre in York. 'The only explanation I can give is that I must have had previous lives,' said the Welsh housewife.

CHAPTER FOUR
Prophets and Seers

Those who can foretell the future are not restricted to bearded sages and withered hags. Pretty young women have sometimes been found capable of the most uncanny predictions. When the words of prophecy seem too grim it is as well to remember that prognostication is about what *could* happen, not only what will happen.

Nostradamus

Reading the prophecies of Nostradamus is not a comfortable experience for twentieth-century man. The legendary French seer, who was proved time and time again to have an awesome gift for predicting the future, forecast that in 1999 our world would be shattered by global conflict in a war to end all wars. Four hundred years ago he wrote:

'In the year 1999 and seven months
From the sky will come the great king of terror . . .
Before and afterward war reigns happily.'

He seems to indicate, however, that the war, which will take place in the Northern Hemisphere, will involve two great powers in an alliance against the East:

'When those of the Northern Pole
are united together
In the East will be great fear and dread.
One day the two great leaders will be friends
The New Land [America] will be at the height of its powers
To the man of blood the number is repeated.'

'The man of blood' is identified elsewhere as being the world's third anti-Christ who will emerge in China. Thus, surprisingly, Nostradamus seems to be suggesting a war between that country and a Russian-American alliance. And after it is over?

'For forty years the rainbow shall not appear.

For forty years it shall be seen every day

The parched earth shall wax drier and drier,

And a great flood when it shall appear.'

This, he seems to forecast, would be the wasteland resulting from a nuclear war. He permits us one glimmer of hope. Before all hell breaks loose 'the Heavens shall show signs', perhaps giving mankind a chance to turn back from his folly.

Surveying our century from four hundred years ago, Nostradamus also predicted strife in the Middle East which would bring a Moslem rebellion against the Christian West; he wrote of the Iraq–Iran war and of how 'the city of Hashem' [Beirut] would be 'attacked by numerous armies and destroyed'. He is credited with having prophesied the atom bomb attacks on Hiroshima and Nagasaki in 1945.

Many of his predictions are stated in quite clear terms, even mentioning people by name, whereas others are phrased in such general terms that even the most devoted Nostradamus scholars sometimes disagree on their interpretation. But his reputation as Europe's greatest prophet rests on the number of times he was proved right, both in his own lifetime and beyond.

Nostradamus was born in Provence on December 14, 1503. His real name was Michel de Nostredame. He decided to change it to the Latin form when he was a student at university. His family was of Jewish descent, but their conversion to Christianity meant young Michel was brought up in the Catholic faith. His grandfathers undertook his education between them, teaching him classical languages, Hebrew and astrology. As an adolescent he studied philosophy at Avignon, then he went on to the University of Montpellier, where he took up medicine, proving himself a brilliant scholar. His fame as a doctor spread rapidly during an outbreak of plague, when he saved many patients who had been regarded by other doctors as incurable. Some of his success was undoubtedly due to his refusal to 'bleed' patients who were desperately ill — a revolutionary idea in the medical world of the early 16th century.

He had seen so much suffering during the plague that he began to search for a deeper insight into the meaning of life by reading every book he could lay hold of on alchemy, magic and the occult. Academic life proved too restricting, so he set out to travel throughout France in a quest for knowledge. He eventually settled in the town of Agen, where he married a young woman of aristocratic blood and went on to raise a family, but when the plague paid another visit to France it claimed his young wife and children as victims. With all his medical skills he had not been able to save them. Bowed with grief, his mind in a turmoil, he set out once again on his search for Truth.

After six years wandering in France, Corsica and Italy he returned to Provence in 1547 and settled down at Salon, where he married a rich widow. It was here his prophetic gift first came to light in written form.

In 1550 Nostradamus published an almanac containing predictions for the coming year, which proved to be so uncannily accurate that people begged him to produce another. He went on turning out almanacs year by year, but his prophetic vision had become so great that it could not be contained in annual predictions. He had in mind a far grander scheme: a complete series of prophecies dealing with events from his own time until the end of the world in the year 7,000. The prophecies were to be divided into ten books, all simply entitled *Centuries*, each volume containing one hundred predictions. They were to be written mostly in quatrains — that is, verses of four lines — their meaning obscured in order to prevent him being accused of witchcraft and brought before the Inquisition. He used a mixture of anagrams, symbols and Old French, as well as deliberately confusing the dated order of the prophecies, but scholars throughout the years have managed to decode his work. Only in the more obscure quatrains have they disagreed as to meaning. Nostradamus left posterity a picture of himself at work in one of his quatrains:

'Seated at night in my secret study
Alone, reposing over the brass tripod,
A slender flame leaps out of the solitude
Making me pronounce that which is not vain.'

Using an instrument similar to the forked rod still employed today for the purpose of divining, he would crouch over a bowl of water on a brass tripod and gaze into its depths as the rod dipped and swerved. From the movement of the rod around the bowl, which was divided into astrological segments, he would divine the future. The 'slender flame' he refers to is the moment of prophetic inspiration. Bowl and rod were used in much the same way that a fortune teller uses a crystal ball, merely to concentrate his powers.

His reputation was established in his own day by several incidents which demonstrated his remarkable mystic vision. While travelling through Italy, for instance, he fell on his knees before a young Franciscan monk called Felice Peretti and addressed him as 'Your Holiness.' Both the monk and those who witnessed this extraordinary behaviour were astounded. But in 1585 that same monk (who had become Cardinal Peretti) was elected Pope Sixtus V. Later, when Nostradamus lived in Salon, he was visited by Queen Catherine de Medici, one of his greatest admirers. The prophet was drawn towards a pale-faced boy in her entourage, singled him out and pronounced that one day he would be king. The boy was Henry of Navarre, who became Henry IV of France.

One of his most famous prophecies concerned Queen Catherine's husband, Henry II of France. Four years before his death he saw precisely how it would happen. Everyone at Court knew of the prediction but dare not speak of it aloud. Nostradamus wrote:

'The young lion shall overcome the old one
In martial field by a single duel,
In a golden cage shall be put out his eye
Two wounds from one, then shall he die a cruel death.'

The 'young lion' was an officer called Montgomery, captain of the French King's Scottish Guard who while jousting with Henry ('the old lion') in a tournament, accidentally pierced the monarch's golden helmet with his lance, putting out his eye and penetrating his brain. The King died after ten days of agony, thus fulfilling the 'cruel death'.

The death of another king, England's Charles I, was vividly described in several verses. Nostradamus spoke of how 'the fortress near the Thames' would fall, 'then the King that was kept within, shall be seen near the bridge in his shirt. . . .' In fact Charles was taken to Windsor Castle, overlooking the Thames, after his defeat by Parliamentary forces in December 1648. A few weeks later, wearing a white shirt, he was taken out and beheaded. In another verse Nostradamus wrote:

'The Parliament of London will put their King to death.
He will die because of the shaven heads in council. . . .'

Clearly the prophet was referring to the Roundheads whom he despised, saying that Cromwell was 'more like a butcher than an English king.' He was quite certain that the Great Plague of London in 1665 was divine punishment for the execution of Charles:

'The Great Plague of the maritime city
Shall not cease until the death be revenged
Of the just blood by price condemned without crime . . .'

He foresaw the Great Fire of London which swept through the capital the following year with such clarity that for once he gave a precise date, leaving out the first two digits as was his custom. 'The blood of the just shall be dry in London', he wrote. 'Burnt by the fire of three times twenty and six.'

Napoleon, the man whom Nostradamus considered the first anti-Christ (Hitler being the second and the third yet to appear on the world scene), is spoken of many times in the books as though Nostradamus could not rid his mind of the man who would bring France almost to her knees because of his ambition. In the first *Century* he refers to Napoleon's birth in Corsica, then an Italian possession:

'An Emperor shall be born in Italy
Who shall cost the Empire dear,

They shall say, with what peoples he keeps company!
He shall be found less a Prince than a butcher.'

Later the prophet saw with equal clarity the tragic fate of the little Corsican whose meteoric rise to power changed the course of history:

'The Great Empire will soon be exchanged for a small place,
    which will soon begin to grow,
    A small place of tiny area in the middle of which
    He will come to lay down his sceptre.'

In fact Napoleon was stripped of his 'great Empire' and exiled to the small island of Elba in 1814, but the following year he escaped and for one hundred days sought to regain his power. His end came when he was seized for a second time and sent to imprisonment and death on the tiny island of St Helena in the South Atlantic.

Nostradamus actually named the second anti-Christ in his predictions, getting the name right except for one letter. He referred to him as Hister instead of Hitler. The reference occurs in a verse thought to describe the early years of the Second World War when German armies swept across the Rhine into France:

'Beast wild with hunger will cross the rivers,
    The great part of the battlefield [the Allies]
    Will be against Hister.'

The prophet foresaw both the beginning and the end of Adolf Hitler in this incredible verse:

'In the mountains of Austria near the Rhine
    There will be born of simple parents
    A man who will claim to defend Poland and Hungary
    And whose fate will never be certain.'

He told of weapons the like of which the world had never seen before and 'machines of flying fire', referring to bombers and the early V weapons. He also foresaw Hitler's treatment of the Jews in concentration camps and their death in the infamous ovens:

'The exiles that were carried into the Isles,
    At the whim of a most cruel monarch [Hitler]
    Shall be murdered, and put in the sparks of fire. . . .'

For once Nostradamus leaves the subject of man's infinite capacity for self-destruction when he speaks of a romance which caused a king to lose his throne — the abdication of Edward VIII, brought about because of his love for the divorced American Mrs Wallis Simpson. In one verse he says:

'For not wanting to consent to the divorce
    Which afterwards will be recognized as unworthy,
    the King of the islands will be forced to flee
    And one put in his place who has no sign of kingship.'

The last line refers to the Duke of York, who, though he had no training or experience, took over his brother's throne and became

George VI when Edward and Mrs Simpson slipped quietly into exile in France:

'A kingdom in dispute and divided between the brothers
To take the arms and the Britannic name,
And the English title. He shall advise himself late
Surprised in the night and carried into the French air.'

There seems to be no part of our history about which Nostradamus did not have some glimmer of knowledge. Returning to our own part of the 20th century, he foretold not only great conflict between Arabs and Jews but between Islam and the West. Some interpreters believe he referred to the conflict in Northern Ireland in a verse which begins 'Before the coming of the ruin of the Celts', and that he foresaw the Falklands War in a prophecy which reads:

'After a naval combat, England will know her greatest alarm.
Then the Soviet adversary will pale with fear
Having sown terror in the Atlantic (or the Atlantic Alliance)'

Nostradamus predicted great social upheaval before the end of our century in which all the old orders would be changed. He prophesied that the reappearance of Halley's Comet in 1985 would bring profound changes in human destiny. But for those of us who survive into the twenty-first century there is, he promises, a thousand years of peace, a Utopian world in which man will forsake aggression and war.

The prophet predicted his own death in 1566, and before it happened he went to an engraver in Salon asking him to engrave a date on a small metal plate, and instructing him that it should be placed in his coffin. In 1700 it was decided to move the coffin from the grave where it had laid for 134 years and move it to a more prominent site. Before it was lowered into the earth for the rest of eternity, those present decided to open the coffin. All that was left of Nostradamus was his skeleton, but on his chest lay the metal plate. The date engraved was 1700.

Jeane Dixon

The violence that cut down three brothers of the Kennedy family was foreseen by Jeane Dixon, America's famous modern seer. The beautiful, dark-haired prophetess predicted the assassination of two of them and the tragic accident that nearly killed the third.

Eleven years before his death she had a psychic vision of John F. Kennedy as she knelt in church one day. She saw an outline of the

White House, a tall, blue-eyed young man with a thick shock of brown hair standing in front of it and the numerals 1–9–6–0. A voice told her that a Democrat who would be inaugurated as President in 1960 would be assassinated while in office.

When John Kennedy was duly elected and became, many felt, a new symbol of hope Jeane Dixon prayed that her prophecy would prove to be wrong. But whenever she looked into the crystal ball which she used to concentrate her power, she saw a huge, black cloud over the White House. In the summer of 1963, when the Kennedys' infant son, Patrick, lost his brief struggle for survival, people asked her if that was the reason for the cloud. She said it was not.

As the year drew on towards November the dark cloud in her vision began to descend on the White House. There was talk of Kennedy going to Dallas. She felt compelled to speak out, to warn someone. She knew that Kay Halle, daughter of Cleveland philanthropist Samuel Halle, was a close friend of the Kennedy family. One day she made an appointment to see her.

'The President has just made a decision to go to some place in the South — you must get word to him not to take the trip,' Mrs Dixon said urgently. 'I know he will be killed. You must warn him.' Kay Halle was embarrassed. She knew Mrs Dixon was highly regarded as a seer, but she also knew that the Kennedy family had no time for psychics. She could not bring herself to deliver the message.

On November 22, 1963, the President and his wife flew to Dallas, Texas, and Jeane Dixon arranged to meet a friend for lunch in Washington. Somehow she had lost her appetite. She could not eat a thing. When, amidst great uproar, news went round the restaurant that someone had shot Kennedy she covered her face with her hands and said to her friend, 'He is dead.' When people protested he was only wounded she repeated 'No, he is dead.' After it was all over she admitted, 'I have never had anything overpower me like this vision.'

Within three months of the assassination of President Kennedy by Lee Harvey Oswald, she knew another blow was coming for the stricken family. She begged someone to warn the handsome young Senator Edward Kennedy to stay away from private aeroplanes for at least two weeks. But the morning after her prophecy news was announced that 'Teddy' had been gravely injured in a chartered plane crash. His back was broken.

Forewarning of the death of Robert Kennedy, who had been so close to the President, came to her in a startling way. She was addressing a convention at the Ambassador Hotel in Los Angeles when a questioner from the floor asked if she thought Robert Kennedy would become President himself one day. Suddenly she saw a black curtain fall between her and the audience. Shaken, she answered, 'No, he will not. He will never be President because of a tragedy that will take place right here in this hotel.' A week later, Robert Kennedy was gunned down at the Ambassador.

Jeane Dixon must be the most glamorous seer in the history of prophecy. Small, slim, with dark hair and blue-green eyes, at one time she used to carry her crystal ball to appointments tucked under her ranch mink coat. She is married to wealthy businessman James Dixon, and she lives in an impressive house with marble floors and antique French furniture, sleeping in a canopied bed once owned by the Empress Eugénie. Strictly vegetarian, she neither smokes nor drinks and attends church every morning. Many great seers have had the same abstemious pattern of life.

She was born Jeane Pinckert in a Wisconsin lumbering village in 1918, but moved to California early in her childhood. She was told by a gypsy that she had the gift of prophecy. When she was only nine she met a lady called Marie Dressler who was thinking of opening a boarding house because she was having no luck as an actress. The little girl looked into the crystal ball she had been given as a plaything and saw sparkling lights and dollar bills. She told her parents. They urged Marie Dressler to go on with her stage career. When she became one of the great names of cinema between the wars the actress remembered the nine-year-old's prediction and said she might never have had a career but for her.

When Jeane left school she went to work in a real estate office, proving herself a first-class business-woman. Stories of her psychic ability spread quickly. During the Second World War she was having her hair set in Westmore's Beauty Salon in Los Angeles when Carole Lombard, the beautiful blonde actress wife of Clark Gable, strolled in. As they were introduced she felt a warning vibration and begged her not to go anywhere by plane for six weeks. The actress replied that she had to leave almost immediately on a tour to promote the sale of war bonds. She laughingly tossed a coin to see whether or not to fly. The coin came down heads, she took her plane to the Mid-west and was killed when it crashed without ever reaching its destination.

After her marriage Jeane Dixon moved to Washington, where she established herself as a prophet on world affairs to whom some of the most powerful men in the world were prepared to listen. America's wartime President, Franklin Delano Roosevelt, summoned her to the White House. He was not the first President to consult a psychic. Abraham Lincoln was persuaded by his wife to send for a young medium called Nettie Colburn when he was anxious about the state of the nation. Mrs Dixon and Roosevelt talked about many things, and when he asked her bluntly how long he had to live she answered with equal frankness but refused to give the date of his death. She correctly predicted that China would turn communist at a time when most people thought that ideology totally alien to the Chinese way of thought.

Jeane Dixon in her husband's real estate office

Roosevelt enjoyed their meetings. 'Take good care of the ball,' he would say with a twinkle when she left him.

She became deeply interested in politics, and with her husband frequently attended embassy parties and developed friendships with several ambassadors. One afternoon in 1945 at a reception given by the Agent General for India, she met a military attaché, Nawabjaba Sher Ali, who asked her for a private reading. She received the soldier at her office and after looking into her crystal ball told him that a partition of India would take place within two years. He protested that no such thing could ever happen but she forecast the date it was announced — February 20, 1947.

Several years later Earl Jellicoe, visiting the British Embassy in Washington, invited her for lunch and asked how she could possibly have foreseen the partition of India two years before it happened. She told him the date had appeared quite clearly in the crystal ball. The numerals were as distinct as the prices listed on their menu. She also added that people from the East were much easier to 'read' than westerners because they did not put up such strong mental barriers.

Ruth Montgomery in *A Gift of Prophecy*, her biography of Jeane Dixon, tells how she forecast her own mother's death. While on a business trip to New York with her husband she had a premonition that they were going to experience a tragedy in the family. At dinner she could hardly eat. 'Death is very near me,' she said. 'It is either my mother or my father.' When they returned to the hotel where they were staying there was a telegram informing them that her mother had died suddenly from a blood clot on the brain.

Over the next few decades her predictions were read nationwide, sometimes in a syndicated column seen by millions of people. Her prophecies continued to be quite remarkable. When she met Winston Churchill in Washington in 1945 she told him that he would be out of office after the war but back in power by 1952. The great man retorted, 'You're wrong. Britain will never let me down.' But she was proved right. She foresaw the assassination of Mahatma Gandhi by a Hindu fanatic in 1948 and the rise in Egypt years later of another great leader, President Sadat.

By the sixties she had become so well known that letters from Europe and Asia addressed simply 'Jeane Dixon, U.S.A.' reached her without any trouble. She made many startling predictions about that decade including the explosion of racial violence in the South, which she rightly warned would grow to such terrible proportions that there would be rioting in the streets. She accurately foretold the death of Dag Hammarskjöld, secretary-general of the United Nations, in a plane crash and also "saw" long before it happened the suicide of Marilyn Monroe. The death of that beautiful and tragic star came to her in a 'psychic flash'.

Jeane Dixon has always been extremely devout and believes that the gift of prophecy comes from God. Once she was asked whether the constant revelations of tragedy did not sometimes weigh heavily on her. She said she did not let them. The only time she was really upset for an extended period was when she knew that President Kennedy was going to be assassinated and could do nothing to stop it.

She has won fame as a crystal gazer but some of her most remarkable premonitions were revealed by unsought visions. . . . Four years before the great Ecumenical Council called by Pope John in 1962 she had a fantastic vision in church one day. Reaching into her purse for coins to buy candles, she found her hands entangled in a mass of purple and gold balls. They floated upward and merged into a massive purple disc edged with gold. The most glorious sunshine flooded the church, and suddenly it was overflowing with people of every nation. When it was over she felt a wonderful sense of peace and completeness.

From experience Jeane Dixon found that the early hours before daybreak provided the clearest channels for psychic meditation. She gets up sometimes at two or three in the morning and sits in the darkness waiting for the dawn, crystal ball ready in front of her.

For this present generation her prophecy is as chilling as that of Nostradamus four centuries earlier: a great war breaking out in the 1980s and a new era of peace starting in 1999. But it is a comfort to know a few of her predictions that have not turned out to be right so far. Russia did not invade Iran or Palestine; China has not used germ warfare against the USA and the Vietnamese war lasted longer than her predicted ninety days. Better to hope she is right when she speaks of a great new world leader rising up in the East towards the end of this millennium, 'a leader who will draw all nations together'.

Joanna Southcott

Devonshire farmer's daughter Joanna Southcott was an eccentric eighteenth-century prophet who formed her own religious sect and at the age of sixty-four announced she was about to give birth to the new Messiah. One of her most bizarre prophecies was that only 144,000 souls would be admitted to paradise when the day of judgment arrived, but she assured her followers they could be certain of gaining entry with the signed and sealed certificates she offered them.

Two hundred years after her death her name has still not been forgotten, largely because of the mysterious affair of what has become known as 'Joanna Southcott's Box'. It was first heard of when a group of her latter-day admirers formed the Panacea Society at the beginning of this century. They announced that the prophet had left a sealed and corded box of writings that could only be opened by a convocation of the twenty-four bishops of England and Wales. Once the seal was broken such things as 'crime, distress and banditry' would disappear from the land. But, warned Joanna, if the convocation never met and the box remained sealed, mankind was doomed.

There are still Southcottians in England today, the Panacea Society, which study her works. They assure the world there is a box in existence, that the one opened by psychical researcher Harry Price in 1927 was not the right one and that there will be no peace until the bishops agree to meet.

Joanna was born at Gittisham, Devonshire, in April 1750, and as a girl worked in the dairy of her father's farm. He thought her too religious, and when her mother died sent her out to service. She worked in various households before gaining a post in Exeter, where she attended both the cathedral and the Wesleyan chapel as often as possible each Sunday. She was pressed to join the Methodists, and did so at Christmas 1791, upsetting the congregation by claiming she had arrived in their midst 'by divine command'.

She was forty-two the following year when, at an Easter meeting, she stood up and made some startling claims for herself. Her fellow Methodists, thinking she had a fever, advised her to go home and rest. She went to stay with her married sister at Plymtree and it was there after ten days in which she experienced 'the powers of darkness' that she began to write her prophesies.

They were put down in a mixture of rambling prose, full of spelling mistakes and peculiar grammar. To give her writings importance she hit upon the idea of sealing them up and forbidding anyone to open them until the predicted events had taken place. She used a small oval seal which she had found among rubbish in a shop where she used to work. It carried the initials 'I C' with a star above and below.

She returned to Exeter, broke with the Methodists, and in 1793 when some of her prophecies were beginning to come true began to demand recognition. She pestered clergymen to examine her claims, but vicars and bishops alike were wary of her. Convinced now she could see into the future, she continued to write her predictions year by year and seal them up, to be read at the appropriate time.

It was not until January 1801, when she issued her first publication, *The Strange Effects of Faith*, that people outside Exeter began to take any notice of her. Colonel Basil Bruce, whose father was vicar of Inglesham in Wiltshire, became her first convert of importance. He introduced her writings to several clergymen and other earnest gentlemen, and they descended on Exeter and after a 'trial' of her writings became her ardent disciples.

She moved to London in May 1802, settled at High House, Paddington, and zealously began to gather followers and build up her ministry. As she had received 'knowledge' that only 144,000 souls were eligible for eternal salvation she decided to issue sealed certificates to her own faithful. These certificates — printed sheets, bearing her oval seal in red wax — proclaimed: 'The sealed of the Lord — the elect precious man's redemption — to inherit the tree of life — to be made heirs of God and joint heirs with Jesus Christ — Joanna Southcott.'

By 1805, when 10,000 of these certificates had been issued, rumours began to circulate that she had made money out of selling salvation. The accusation was probably false. However, the bottom certainly fell out of the market in 1809 when a particularly nasty murderess called Mary Bateman was hanged at York, pronouncing herself to be a certificate holder!

Joanna continued to hold 'trials' or public debates of her prophecies at her home in Paddington. Wealthy people were often invited and received personal messages for which they made handsome contributions to the cause. She began to set up chapels for her followers in which she used the Anglican prayer book and preached fairly orthodox theology. One Southcottian chapel opened in Bermondsey, East London. It was established after her meeting with Henry Prescott, an apprentice who was generally known as 'Joseph' because of his marvellous and prophetic dreams. She interpreted his dreams for him and had them depicted on the chapel walls.

Travelling north, she set up chapels in Salford, Leeds and Stockton-on-Tees. Some extremely odd people were attracted to her. One Southcottian leader, for instance, a man named Benjamin Smith, threw himself from Blackfriars Bridge in London, fully expecting that angels would catch him. He hit his head on a stone buttress and perished.

But the most bizarre part of her ministry was still to come. At the age of sixty-four she announced in her *Third Book of Wonders* that she was to become the mother of 'Shiloh', the new Messiah, and she intended to go into retreat and wait for the birth. From October 11, 1813, she shut herself away from society in the house she now owned in Manchester Street, London. She saw only the two faithful female friends who lived with her, Jane Townley and Ann Underwood. Every bishop, peer and member of parliament she could think of received a personal letter from her telling them the glad news. She also informed *The Times* and *Morning Herald*. She expected 'Shiloh' to be born, she said, some time in the following year.

Joanna became ill on March 17, 1814, but it was not until August 1 that Jane Townley thought it necessary to call in the doctors. Nine prominent medical men attended her and were baffled. Some of them admitted that had she been a younger woman they would have concluded from her symptoms that she was four months pregnant.

There was great rejoicing among Joanna's followers when the news leaked out. They ordered a crib from Seddons of Aldersgate Street, silver feeding spoons and a superbly bound Bible, hand-tooled and blocked in gold leaf. A 'great personage' offered the Temple of Peace in Green Park as a suitable place for the confinement. When Dr Richard Reece visited her on November 19, however, Joanna told him that she was gradually dying and directed him to open her body four days after death.

On her instructions all the gifts prepared for 'Shiloh' were returned, and though Dr Reece could find nothing wrong with her she grew weaker and weaker until on December 27, 1814, she died. An autopsy was performed as she had wished. There was no sign of a physical pregnancy, no functional disorder or disease. Joanna Southcott had obviously gone through what we now call an 'hysterical' or 'phantom' pregnancy brought on by her desire to be mother of the new Messiah.

She was buried in St John's Wood Cemetery with a tombstone bearing the line 'Thou'lt appear in greater power.' When the stone was shattered by a huge explosion in Regent's Park in 1874 her followers hoped that it was a sign she would return again. The mystery of Joanna Southcott's box remains to intrigue another generation. The one that Harry Price opened contained, he alleged, nothing more than an old nightcap, a pistol and various oddments, none of them belonging to Joanna. The whereabouts of the real one remains a secret.

Mother Shipton

One of the most famous tourist sights in Yorkshire lies in the ancient town of Knaresborough on the River Nidd. There, enfolded in magnificent scenery, is a well with petrifying waters and Mother Shipton's cave, once the haunt of a legendary prophetess.

Ursula Sontheil — or Mother Shipton, as she became better known — was a sibyl who could look so far into the future that in the mid-16th century she prophesied:

'Carriages without horses shall go
And accidents shall fill the world with woe.'

And, anticipating the first modern telegraph of 1837, she promised her contemporaries:

'Around the world thoughts shall fly
In the twinkling of an eye.'

She looked like a witch with her misshapen body, crooked legs, strange goggling eyes and crooked nose, but it was said that any person who met or talked with her came away with the greatest respect for the odd little creature.

According to local legend she inherited her powers of clairvoyance from her mother. Agatha Sontheil was a wild creature, left an orphan at an early age and forced to earn her living by begging. Wandering through the Knaresborough woods one day, she met a young man of aristocratic bearing. They became lovers. Not only did he provide her with more than enough money for her needs but, says the legend, he announced that he was no ordinary mortal and would give her extraordinary powers, including the gift of prophecy.

Whatever the truth, people flocked to see her whenever she returned from her wanderings with the young man. On one occasion, the story goes, she was so angered by their curiosity that she invoked the aid of the winds and they were blown back into their own homes. This, and similar incidents, led to her being brought before the local justices on a charge of witchcraft, but she was acquitted.

Agatha gave birth to her daughter Ursula in July 1488 — 'Near this petrifying well I first drew breath, as records tell.' She was an ugly, deformed infant, and after producing her Agatha retired to a convent, where she soon died.

Ursula Sontheil was put into the care of the parish nurse, who found the task of looking after her more than she could manage. Eventually it was decided to send her to school, where she would be submitted to harsh discipline. Her teachers were surprised to find that she learned to read and write more easily than any of the other children, and demonstrated a quick intelligence. She was subjected to cruel taunts in the playground because of her deformities. In return, it was claimed, she used witchcraft to punish her tormentors so that they felt themselves pulled, pinched and hauled about even when she stood apart from them. Ursula was sent away from school for this reason and never educated again.

Little is known of her youth and early married life except that she became the wife of Toby Shipton from Shipton, near York, when she was twenty-four. She set up home in a respectable way, but as soon as it became known that she could see into the future people from all around flocked to her doorstep. At first she devoted her gifts to purely local matters such as predicting births, marriages and deaths, but it soon became obvious that her range of prophecy was greater than that, and she began to turn her attention to affairs of the world.

Mother Shipton (as she was known from now on) always prophesied in symbolic language. Her first great prophecy of European significance was recorded in the following words:

'When the English Lion shall set his feet on Gallic shore
Then shall the lilies begin to droop for fear.
There shall be much weeping and wailing among the ladies of that country
Because the princely Eagle shall join with the Lion to tread all that shall oppose them.'

The English Lion was Henry VIII of England, who in 1513 landed on the Gallic shore with a total force of 50,000 men. Lilies are the national emblem of France, and Henry's invasion did indeed create great fear. The princely Eagle was Maximilian, the German emperor who joined forces with Henry to overcome the French.

After Henry's victory in France Mother Shipton turned her attention to the great Cardinal Wolsey, who she called 'The Mitred Peacock', and foretold exactly what would happen when the proud prelate's wealth and influence began to equal that of the king himself.

'The Mitred Peacock now shall begin to plume himself

And his train shall make a great show in the world.
He shall want to live at York, and shall see it, but shall never come thither
And finally, after great misfortunes he shall finish with Kingston.'
Mother Shipton's prophecy with regard to his never seeing York was fulfilled, for though he held that bishopric, in addition to several others, he was prevented from going there when his 'great train' was stopped and he was arrested for high treason. After much humiliation he came into the care of Sir William Kingston, Constable of the Tower of London.

She foresaw the dissolution of the monasteries years before Henry VIII issued his ruthless orders, and rightly predicted the suffering of the poor who would no longer be cared for by monks. Looking further into the future, she predicted, as several other prophets did also, that traumatic event in English history, the execution of Charles I.

'The Crown then fits the White King's head
Who with the lilies soon shall wed;
Then shall a peasant's bloody knife
Deprive a great man of his life.'

The White King was Charles I, robed in white for his coronation. The lilies are a symbol of his French bride, Henrietta Maria, daughter of Henry IV of France.

Mother Shipton's prophetic verse covered page after page in symbolic couplets as she caught glimpses of a future she would never see. 'Men shall walk over rivers and under rivers, Iron in the water shall float', she predicted.

She foretold the death of that pathetic little Queen, Jane Grey 'a virtuous lady then shall die, For being raised up too high' and the defeat of the Spanish Armada 'And the Western Monarch's wooden horses, Shall be destroyed by Drake's forces'. Sir Walter Raleigh's popularization of the tobacco plant and the potato was predicted in the following lines:

'Over a wild and stormy sea
Shall a noble sail
Who to find will not fail
A new and fair countree
From whence he shall bring
A herb and a root. . . .'

A long time before her death Mother Shipton told her friends the day and hour when she would take her departure. Exactly to time in the year 1561 she took solemn leave of all those near to her, lay down on her bed and died. She was seventy-three.

Her memory is still honoured today, especially in Yorkshire. A stone has been erected to her memory near Clifton about a mile from the City of York.

John Dee

John Dee was the sixteenth century's 007, a man shrewd and sophisticated enough to be secret agent, spy and 'noble intelligencer' to Queen Elizabeth I. Yet this same man also claimed that he had found a way to talk to the angels and knew what went on in heaven.

Dee was given the code number 007 — also chosen by Ian Fleming for his popular fictional spy, James Bond — when he was sent to the Continent to find out what was going on in foreign diplomatic circles. The Queen called him 'my ubiquitous eyes'. But at the same time Dee was immersed in occult activities which rendered him trance-like, and made pronouncements that made his enemies regard him as a credulous fool.

John Dee was a scholar, highly revered for his work on mathematics and navigation, but besides being a man of science he also accepted the existence of a sixth sense which could emerge spontaneously in dreams, visions or intuitions. Through this sixth sense he believed he had learned the secrets of the angels, and knew which of them controlled various parts of the world. He also believed he had caught a glimpse of future traumatic events when in a trance-like state.

He looks out at us from sixteenth-century portraits with brooding, smouldering eyes. His beard is long, white and pointed and he wears a deep white ruff and a black cap. He was born on July 13, 1527, at Mortlake, which was then a pleasant village on the outskirts of London. An intense young man with a passion for books, he became an undergraduate at Cambridge when he was only fifteen, and got into the habit of sleeping only four hours a night so that he might study more. His efforts were rewarded when, before the age of twenty, he was also made a Fellow of the newly founded Trinity College. Even at this early stage of his career it was rumoured that Dee dabbled in witchcraft and was somewhat eccentric.

For the next thirty years he travelled widely in Europe, lecturing at universities and building up his reputation as a mathematical scholar and astrologer. He was said to have been largely responsible for the revival of interest in mathematics in England in the sixteenth century, and his work on navigation has earned him a place in all the reference books. But John Dee was as deeply engrossed with the magic formula for invoking Venus as he was with mathematical equations, charts and maps. He became intensely interested in the 'angelic magic' introduced by a priest called Abbot Trithemius in a scholarly work entitled *Steganographia*. He also cast the horoscopes of the great men and women of his time, and was unwise enough in 1554 to forecast when the reign of

Mary Tudor, who was on the English throne, would come to an end.

At this time Mary's half-sister, the Princess Elizabeth, was under house arrest, suspected of plotting with Thomas Wyatt in a rebellion against the Catholic Queen's rule of terror. Through one of her ladies-in-waiting the young Princess, hungry for intellectual companionship, began a correspondence with Dee. One day he sent her his horoscope for Queen Mary. It was discovered by two informers in Elizabeth's household and the letters between the young Princess and the scholarly astrologer were reported to Mary's Council.

Dee was immediately arrested and, suspected of plotting Mary Tudor's death by black magic, thrown into prison. 'They believe me to be a companion of hellhounds and a caller and conjurer of wicked spirits', he wrote to a friend, deeply distressed. He insisted that his acceptance of the sixth sense and his attempts to tap the powers that existed had nothing to do with witchcraft. He told Lord Burghley — who was to become Elizabeth's great Principal Secretary of State — that 'some people, like himself, had supernormal powers not of a magician but of a peculiar and scientific quality.'

Dee was eventually cleared of high treason but on his release was immediately rearrested and clapped into prison again, this time on the charge of being a heretic. No one could prove heresy and he finally gained his freedom at the end of 1555.

For some years he contented himself with scientific research and experiment. His library was famous throughout England, being exceptionally large for the period and containing books and manuscripts on every subject under the sun.

When Mary Tudor died in 1558 and Elizabeth ascended to the throne, John Dee came into his own. Always loyal and generous to those she considered had served her well, Elizabeth rewarded Dee for his past services by making him her personal astrological adviser. It was Dee who selected a propitious date for her coronation; he who was called upon for advice when she suspected that sorcery was being used against her. At the same time, realizing his shrewd understanding of all that was going on in Europe, she created him her secret agent 007 and sent him off on spying missions to foreign Courts.

Because Dee was such a favourite with the Queen he was allowed to carry on with his occult experiments. He used techniques that sometimes demanded the use of a divining rod, at other times a pendulum. In 1580 he began to experiment with different occult methods. 'I had a sight offered me in a crystal this day,' he wrote in his diary. He became increasingly absorbed in the 'angelic magic' expounded by the Abbot Trithemius and in October 1581 began his attempts to communicate with the angels. Perhaps, it has been suggested, the spirits were trying to get in touch with him. His sleep had been increasingly disturbed, his dreams strange, and there were mysterious knockings and rappings going on in his house for which he could not account.

He worked through several mediums, including a Greek peasant woman, but eventually in March 1582 he found Edward Kelley. This strange young man, who was only twenty-seven when Dee met him, had packed his short life full of mystery and dubious adventures. He had started out as a notary but was accused of forgery. He had studied alchemy and had in his possession strange elixirs, powders and cipher manuscripts. It was even rumoured that he practised necromancy, the rite of raising the dead for the purpose of prediction and divination.

Through Kelley, Dee became convinced he was in touch with the heavenly host. The young man obviously had occult powers. But Dee did not trust him. He persuaded the angels to answer in a language called 'Enochian', and according to one of them it was the same that was used in the Garden of Eden. Records of these conversations, compiled by Dee, have survived to this day. The spirit utterances were not particularly illuminating, apart from one passage which apparently records a contact between Dee and the angel Uriel on May 5, 1583:

Dee: As concerning the vision which was presented yesternight (unlooked for) to the sight of Edward Kelley as he sat at supper with me in my hall, I mean the appearing of the very sea and many ships thereon, and the cutting of the head of a woman by a tall, black man, what are we to imagine thereof?

Uriel: The one did signify the provision of foreign powers against the welfare of this land; which they shall shortly put into practice. The other, the death of the Queen of Scots: it is not long unto it.

The angel, speaking through Kelley (who did not understand the Enochian language), was obviously prophesying the attempted invasion of England by the Spanish Armada in 1588 and the execution of Mary, Queen of Scots in 1587.

At first sight John Dee's records seemed to have been written in gibberish, but fellow scholars admitted that 'Enochian' after careful study did show traces of syntax and grammar. To the modern reader they would be almost impossible to decipher as they contained long references to Elizabethan forms of magic and alchemy.

The strange association between the rogue and the scholar lasted for seven years. They held hundreds of séances and the angels who spoke through Kelley seemed determined to keep the men on the move. Acting according to angelic instructions, they wandered all over Europe. By the spring of 1587, however, Kelley was obviously beginning to get bored. After quarrelling with Dee he went off to try his hand at alchemy, hoping to be able to transmute base metals into gold.

John Dee, unable to find another medium who could work with him, returned to England, gave up all his occult practices and returned to mathematics. He seems to have lost touch with the angels. He died in 1608.

CHAPTER FIVE

Spirits and Priestesses

Flamboyant figures who started new movements that have made their impact on the world today and whose followers believe them to have been divinely inspired.

The Fox sisters

The Fox family, living in a small wood-frame house in Hydesville near Rochester in New York state, had not been sleeping at all well. During the last few nights of March 1848 their rest had been constantly disturbed by strange knocks and raps and sounds as though furniture was being moved about. Reluctantly the Fox parents, John and Margaret, came to the conclusion that they had moved into a haunted house.

Of their seven children only the two youngest daughters, Katherine, aged eleven, and Margaretta, thirteen, were still living with them. On the night of Friday, March 31, worn out with disturbed nights, they all retired to bed early.

For once the children were allowed to sleep in their parents' room, so, far from being frightened, when the noises started again the mischievous youngest child, Kate, began to imitate the raps. It became something of a game. Margaretta called out, 'Do just as I do. Count one, two, three, four.' Four raps came in answer. From this the game proceeded to a more advanced stage. The girls hit on the idea of calling out letters of the alphabet and asking the mysterious communicator to rap when a letter was appropriate. By this means simple 'yes' and 'no' were supplemented by whole sentences. After a time the rapper was revealed as the spirit of a 31-year-old peddler who had been murdered in that very house and whose remains were buried in the cellar.

What happened that night to a poor family living in rural America had astounding repercussions. It marked the beginning of the modern Spiritualist movement. The living, it appeared, had communicated with the dead and exchanged information. But, extraordinary as the Hydesville happenings were, they might well have remained a purely local sensation, as Ruth Brandon points out in her book *The Spiritualists*. After all, it was not the first time that spirits of the dead had communicated or purported to communicate with the living using very similar techniques. But America was caught up in the nineteenth-century passion for the occult. And the Fox girls had an older sister, Leah, who was ambitious and meant to make the most of their mysterious rappings.

The morning after Kate and Margaretta made contact with the spirit of the peddler, neighbours flocked to the house to listen and take part in the weird goings-on. They heard raps, put questions of their own and received answers. Some of the men decided to dig up the cellar floor to see if the story could be substantiated, but the ground was waterlogged and they had to abandon their attempts. Later, however, another digging party uncovered parts of a male body. Most people believed the peddler had been found.

Life in the Hydesville house became intolerable as far as the Fox parents were concerned. They were confused and upset by what was going on and seriously wondered at one point whether someone had put a curse on them. After a weekend in which three hundred people descended on Hydesville eager to hear the rapping, they moved out, taking Kate and Margaretta to stay with one of their sons, David.

To their dismay and astonishment, the raps moved with them. For the first time John and Margaret Fox realized that the strange noises were directly connected with their young daughters. The raps occurred only in their presence and wherever they went. Their lives were totally disrupted by the attention and publicity and eventually it was decided to separate the girls to see if the rappings would cease and leave them all in peace. Kate and Mrs Fox went to stay with Leah in Rochester, leaving Margaretta behind with her brother David, but it made no difference.

Leah Fox was a woman who knew how to get things done. Soon both girls were living with her and she hired the biggest hall in town so that they could give a demonstration of their powers. Both girls began to give séances and to produce new phenomena. People felt themselves being touched by spirit hands, objects moved of their own volition, musical instruments played though no one went near them.

They attracted capacity audiences. Public opinion was sharply divided, however, and feelings ran high. The girls were ridiculed, physically attacked and even threatened with death by those who saw them as agents of the devil.

They were asked to submit to an investigation by a committee in Rochester, but when its members could find no evidence of trickery another was set up with instructions to make the tests more difficult. This second committee also failed to produce damning evidence so a third was appointed, this time made up entirely of women so that the sisters could be stripped and searched. But this committee too reported that the girls appeared to be totally genuine and that even when made to stand on pillows with their ankles tied together and their hands secured, the rapping came loud and clear from ceiling, walls and floor.

Two years had passed since the memorable night in Hydesville and it had now become almost impossible for the girls to lead a normal life. They were in constant demand. They left Rochester for the more sophisticated psychic circles of New York, where they gave public performances as professionals as well as private séances for wealthy clients. Many of their 'sitters' were sceptics who would have been only too delighted to reveal to the world how the Fox sisters operated. They emerged admitting that even if they were not convinced by the spirit messages they could not deny that the phenomena defied normal explanation. Horace Greeley, Editor of the *New York Herald-Tribune* and one of the most influential men in America, became their champion.

Then, out of the blue in 1851 came a shattering statement from a Mrs Norman Culver who was a relative by marriage to the Fox sisters. She claimed that Kate herself had confessed to her that both she and Margaretta had learned how to make rapping noises by clicking their toes. There was an uproar as the sceptics gleefully pointed out that they had been right all the time and that the girls were nothing more nor less than a clever vaudeville act. On the other side the girls' supporters were quick to unearth the fact that Mrs Culver had had a bitter quarrel with the girls' parents. Whatever she said was probably motivated by spite. They asked, too, how clicking toe joints could account for the other phenomena and the fact that at their séances and public performances all kinds of other noises were heard, ranging from hammer blows to the sawing of wood.

All through the fifties Leah, the girls' older sister, had been the organizing genius behind everything they did. She made a handsome profit out of them, and though Kate and Margaretta were responsible for the phenomena it was she who managed to gain a reputation as a great medium whose séances were a social event. By the end of the decade she had divorced her husband and married a wealthy New York banker. Her psychic establishment was closed down and she disowned the sisters who had been responsible for her success.

The Fox Sisters

Both had tragic personal lives. Margaretta's marriage to Elisha Kent Kane, the famous Arctic explorer who had courted her, against his family's wishes, since she was thirteen was to end after only a few years when he died far away from her in Cuba. Kate, married to lawyer Henry Jencken in 1872, also lost her husband after a pathetically short marriage, though he left her two children to console her.

Margaretta was destroyed by the loss of her husband and though she half-heartedly gave spiritualist demonstrations in order to earn her living she also began to drink and take drugs. Leah did not want to know her. Kate Fox continued to make her mark as a medium. On a visit to England she was investigated by William (later Sir William) Crookes, the eminent scientist, who introduced her to the most famous medium in England, Daniel Dunglas Home. Usually Home steered clear of other psychics, especially when they insisted on operating in darkness, for he was proud of the fact that no one had ever been able to accuse him of trickery. But he allowed himself to be tested jointly with Kate Fox.

Crookes, who was not complimentary about Kate's intellectual capacity, nevertheless considered her a remarkable medium. He said it was only necessary for her to put her hand on any substance for loud thuds to be heard coming from it, like a triple pulsation sometimes loud enough to be heard several rooms away. 'In this manner I have heard them in a living tree, on a sheet of glass, on a stretched iron wire, on a tambourine on the roof of a cab and on the floor of a theatre.' At her wedding it was said loud raps were heard at the reception and the table on which the wedding cake stood was repeatedly raised from the floor! Kate had nine years of domesticity, then it was all over.

As the years passed both Margaretta and Kate, having lost their husbands, sank together into a life of drunken squalor. Leah was no longer available to organize things for them. Their psychic powers, if they ever had them, seemed to be coming to an end. Then, one momentous day in October 1888 the Fox sisters pulled the rug from under the spiritualist movement, and got their own back on Leah.

Standing up in front of a packed house at the New York Academy of Music, Margaretta confessed that as far as she was concerned spiritualism had been nothing but an imposture from the very beginning. Barefooted, she demonstrated how she could produce raps and cracks with her big toe and the noise echoed loud and clear from the gallery, the back of the hall and the ceiling. Kate, sitting in a box overlooking the stage, said nothing, so it was presumed that she was in full agreement with her sister. A letter she wrote shortly afterwards explained why they had done such an extraordinary thing. They were penniless. The venture had earned them 1,500 dollars.

A few days after her appearance at the Academy Margaretta just as surprisingly retracted what she had said. Desperate for money, she had apparently agreed to collaborate with a journalist who wrote for the *New York World* in order to provide a story, and later a book, which could be headlined 'Death Blow to Spiritualism.' Quite a few people had felt all along that the affair was stage-managed. The sisters would only do themselves harm by such a confession. They felt justified in their suspicions when Margaretta said to another reporter, 'Would to God I could undo the injustice I did the cause of spiritualism. I was under the strong psychological influence of persons inimical to it.'

Sceptics felt sure the movement had been delivered a death blow, but after a sharp intake of breath it went on from strength to strength. The Fox sisters, however, never restored their standing as long as they lived. Their last years were a hopeless mess. Drunk, destitute, now hardly comprehending what they had started all those years ago, they died very soon after each other in 1895, Margaretta going first. They were buried in a pauper's grave.

Their old home in Hydesville started to collapse in 1904 but today a replica housing a museum stands in its place, and on a plaque erected outside marking 'The Birthplace and Shrine of Modern Spiritualism' their names are engraved in stone.

Madame Blavatsky

Search through the history of occult practice and you will find no more dramatic figure than the Russian mystic who was born Helena Petrova Hahn and became known to posterity as Madame Blavatsky. As a child she was constantly drenched with holy water by her Greek Orthodox nurses who thought she was possessed by the devil. As a young woman she stood out among the bizarre sights of Cairo as, dressed as an Arab and smoking hashish, she sat at the feet of occult gurus. In middle age she formed the Theosophical Society, dedicated to spiritual truth, with the help, she claimed, of long-dead Mahatmas (masters) with names like Koot Hoomi and Mahatma Morya. Towards the end of her life she came into a head-on collision with psychical researchers who said she was one of the most accomplished, ingenious and interesting impostors of history, yet at the same time her teachings were heavily influencing a young lawyer called Gandhi.

Helena Petrova Hahn came from a family which bristled with titles. On her mother's side were the blue bloods of generations of Russians, including her maternal grandmother the Princess Helene Dolgorouky. On her father's side she was descended from a noble German family, and her paternal grandfather rejoiced in the name of General Alexis von Rottenstern Hahn. She was born at Ekaterinoslav in the Ukraine on July 31, 1831. From the moment she arrived in the world cataclysmic things happened around her. She was conceived at the same time that cholera reached Russia and her birth took place as people in the same house were dying from the plague. Fire broke out at her baptism when a small cousin, bored with the ceremony and playing with a lighted taper, accidentally set fire to the priest's robe, nearly burning the man to death.

These incidents, taking place as they did in a society riddled with superstition, set her apart. Servants regarded her with awe and allowed her to do what she liked. From the earliest age she showed a terrifying will and strange excitability of temperament. She was liable to ungovernable fits of passion. Only the fact that she was gifted, daring and (when in a good mood) humorous made her bearable.

Her mother died when she was eleven and the young Helena was sent to Saratow, where her grandfather was civil governor, to be brought up by her grandparents. Still a difficult child, given to hypochondria and walking in her sleep, she began showing unmistakable signs of psychic 'peculiarities'. Her Greek Orthodox nurses considered her possessed by the devil, and had her exorcized. Her grandparents' great country house at Saratow was the perfect backcloth for her imagination. Vast, turreted, resembling a medieval castle, it was honeycombed with subterranean passages and long-abandoned galleries. She would sometimes be found walking through the long, dim corridors in deep conversation with someone invisible. Helena believed in spirits. In fact she seems to have had early in life all the characteristics of mediumship as well as the gifts of a clairvoyant.

Friends and relatives at Saratow were half-intrigued, half-frightened by this aspect of her nature. Visitors to the house would sometimes be shocked when after gazing at them intently she proceeded to tell them the date on which they would die or when some accident or misfortune would happen to them. Since her predictions often came true, she was regarded with considerable misgivings as the terror of the family.

Her life at Saratow is known in detail because of the vivid account of it written by her sister, Madame de Jelihowsky. 'She was a strange girl, full of uncontrollable mischief one minute . . . the next she would give it all up to devour books. Her grandparents' enormous library seemed hardly large enough to satisfy her cravings.' She loved to ride high-mettled horses, and by the age of fifteen could manage any Cossack horse on a man's saddle. She defied everyone.

Her defiance led to her first marriage. At seventeen she had plenty of suitors but turned them all down. Her governess, exasperated, said that if she carried on like this even old General Blavatsky, who frequently visited the family, would decline to have her for a wife. The challenge was too tempting for young Helena. She set her cap at the 'plumeless raven' as she secretly called Blavatsky, and though he was fifty years older than her, accepted his proposal.

The marriage lasted barely three months. After a brief, stormy relationship she took one of his horses and galloped off to Tiflis. Her family did not see her again for ten years. Bearing the name by which she would be known to posterity, Madame Blavatsky set out on her wanderings.

There is a story that for a time she worked as a bareback rider in a circus. She certainly contracted a bigamous marriage with the opera singer Metrovitch, and there is reason to believe she bore him a child.

At one point she left him to become an assistant to Daniel Dunglas Home, the great spiritualist medium, but the affair was doomed anyway. In July 1851, they were passengers on board the steamship *Eumonia* when it sank after an explosion in the boiler room. Metrovitch was drowned but Madame Blavatsky was among the survivors picked up by a passing freighter.

The rescue ship put her ashore in Egypt and she made her way to Cairo and began her first serious study of the occult with an old Copt, a magician. From then on her thirst for knowledge was insatiable. Colonel Hahn, her father, who had kept in touch with her ever since her flight from Russia and who secretly admired her spirit, sent her money to continue her travels. She crossed the Atlantic to Canada to study the occult with Red Indians, went on to Mexico, then to New Orleans, where the chief interest of her visit was voodoo. Her American travels lasted for about a year, then she resolved to go to India and try to find a way through Nepal into the forbidden country of Tibet. Her first attempt was frustrated. She wandered on for two more years before making a second. This time with a Tartar 'shaman' or holy man as her guide she succeeded in penetrating a considerable way into the country which then held such mystery for outsiders. She had many strange experiences in the bleak lands of Tibet. On one occasion she said she saw the 'astral soul' of her guide separate from his body. It remained one of the high points of her occult experience, and she said she remembered it clearly to the end of her life. Madame Blavatsky and the shaman had to be rescued from the desert eventually by a party of horsemen from a lamasery, whom she believed had been directed to them by psychic powers. The incident in the desert put an end to her wanderings in Tibet. She was politely escorted back to the frontier.

She returned to India, but shortly before the Mutiny broke out in 1857 she was directed to leave the country by her 'spiritual protector'. After an absence of ten years she made a typically melodramatic return to Russia in the middle of a family wedding party at Pskoff, about 180 miles from St Petersburg. She proceeded to astonish everyone with demonstrations of her gathering psychic powers. Her sister, Madame de Jelihowsky, reported that as soon as she returned to live in the house they were aware of strange things happening in it. Raps and whispering sounds, mysterious and unexplained, were now being heard constantly wherever she went. 'Not only did they occur in her presence and near her but knocks were heard and movements of the furniture perceived in nearly every room of the house.' The house, it seems, was always full of visitors but Madame Blavatsky would sit quietly on a sofa, getting on with her embroidery while the rapping and banging went on around her.

Early in 1859 she went with her father and sister to stay in an old house in the village of Rougodero, near St Petersburg, where they remained for a whole year. During this time she often saw ghosts, which she described in detail. Once she encountered the phantom of an old lady, 'a fat old thing with a frilled white cap, white kerchief across her shoulders, a short, grey narrow dress and checked apron'. Servants identified her as a German who had been housekeeper there for twenty years. She also saw the apparition of an old man, very strange to look at, with a high black headdress and long grey coat. She particularly noticed his terribly long finger-nails. Two peasants identified him as their former master, Shousherin. His long nails, they explained, were the result of a rare disease. One of the effects of this illness is that the nails of the fingers and toes would not be cut without the sufferer bleeding to death.

While she was living quietly with her family she became very ill. Years before, travelling in Asia, she had somehow received a wound just under the heart which occasionally reopened and brought on high fever. The local doctor was sent for but emerged from her bedroom trembling with terror. He swore that as he bent over to examine her the shadow of a hand appeared and moved slowly up and down her body from head to waist, as though forbidding him to touch her. This, combined with the noises that were going on in the room, caused him to take to his heels.

Madame Blavatsky recovered and set out on a visit to her grand-parents in the Caucasus. At Zadonsk, on the way, she and her sister were received by the Holy Metropolitan Isadore, an old friend of the family who had known them since childhood. He received them kindly, but, Madame Jelihowsky reported, they had hardly taken their seats in his drawing room when a terrible hubbub broke out: loud raps (which surprised even Madame Blavatsky) were followed by thumps and cracks all over the room. The chandelier overhead shook its crystal drops, then, on seeing a huge armchair sliding towards him, the Arch-bishop began to laugh outright. He told them he was very interested in these phenomena and had read a great deal about so-called spiritual manifestations. Before they left he blessed them and said to Madame Blavatsky: 'As for you, do not be troubled by the gift you are possessed of, do not let it become a source of misery . . . it was given to you for some purpose . . . use it with discrimination. . . .'

She knew she must return to the East. She went back to India and became a *chela*, a devout student sitting at the feet of gurus and mystics. She felt she was in spiritual touch with the great Mahatmas or masters of Eastern religion, and vowed to serve them for the rest of her life. For years she continued her wanderings, increasing still further her considerable store of occult knowledge.

By the time she decided to return to America in 1873 she was penniless. She hoped to gain patronage from wealthy families interested in psychic matters, but she spent months living in extreme poverty in a New York slum. Eventually she obtained work as a dressmaker and could at least buy food and cheap tobacco to make the cigarettes she smoked endlessly. Not even her desperate circumstances, however, interfered with her passion for the occult. The USA was, she said in a letter written home, 'a most prolific hotbed for mediums and sensitives of all kinds, both genuine and artificial'.

Madame Blavatsky was saved from poverty by the generosity of an American she had met on a previous visit. Soon she began to arrange meetings with other people who were interested in the psychic world. Aspiring to higher things, she also began to protest openly about being called a 'medium'. She did, she admitted, see ghosts when others did not — 'the shadows of terrestrial bodies from which in most cases the soul and spirit had fled long ago'. But she wanted above all to discover the soul, to communicate to the West the great philosophical truths of the East, to make the whole world more aware of spiritual truth.

It was at one of these meetings held at a farmhouse in Vermont owned by the Eddy brothers, two famous American mediums, that she met a man who was to be part of her life from now on — Colonel Henry S. Olcott. From the moment he was introduced to her she had a remarkable effect on him. He found her eccentric but utterly fascinating. The bespectacled, bearded American lawyer decided to throw up his professional career and devote his life to helping this extraordinary Russian present spiritual truth to the world.

Olcott was the one who suggested that she should form a society that could be devoted to studying these things. She agreed, and within a short time the Theosophical Society came into existence. Olcott became its chairman and missionary; Madame Blavatsky opted for the title 'founder' and stayed at headquarters doing secretarial work and writing.

Her relationship with the Colonel was not apparently romantic or sexual, but she could not do without him from now on. He was kind and generous to her, though she often treated him badly. Membership of the Society increased rapidly. Madame Blavatsky now lived in a more spacious apartment in New York, plainly furnished but littered with curios — huge palm leaves, tigers' heads, stuffed apes, oriental pipes and vases, manuscripts and cuckoo clocks. It always seemed to be teeming with people of all nationalities. Madame herself spoke Russian most of the time, shrewdly observing each visitor with what Olcott called her 'mystical blue eyes'. An American who became her friend found her 'from morning till night surrounded by people. Mysterious events, extraordinary sights and sounds continue to occur. I have been there many an evening and seen in broad gas light large luminous balls creeping over the furniture or playfully jumping from point to point while the most beautiful liquid bell sounds now and again burst out from the air of the room.' Madame Blavatsky seems never to have exhibited hysteria or the slightest appearance of trance. She was always in full possession of her faculties while the phenomena were taking place.

The hard life she had led had coarsened her complexion. She peppered her language with expletives, some witty and amusing, some violent. To be suspected as an impostor would bring forth a torrent of passionate abuse against some person or other who had misjudged her or her Society. Many outside her intimate circle found it difficult to believe in her as an exalted moralist trying to lead people to a better spiritual life. But she wrote to her sister: 'I am — heaven help us — becoming fashionable. I am writing articles on Esotericism and Nirvana and am paid for them more than I could ever have expected.'

In his book describing incidents in her life, her devoted disciple and friend, journalist A. P. Sinnett, quoted an article published in the *New York Times* in January 1885. It described her as a woman of remarkable characteristics. 'Those who only knew her slightly', said the writer, 'invariably described her as a charlatan; those who knew her better thought she was a learned but deluded enthusiast; those who knew her intimately were either carried away into a belief in her powers or were profoundly puzzled. . . .'

Her flat became a meeting place for the oddest group of individuals. She published a weighty tome called *Isis Unveiled*, which had a moderate success, and was in the process of becoming quite a cult figure. But it was in India, not the USA, that she felt her future lay and one February day in 1879 she collected a loyal band of disciples together and set off for the East.

The early Theosophists presented an eccentric picture. Their aggressive sympathy for the Hindu population and general contempt for the European set was rather overdone. Madame Blavatsky said she did not wish to be political in any way, but she did not really understand the social problems of the time. She lived almost entirely with the native society in Bombay, which brought her and her party under suspicion. They were put under police surveillance by the British authorities and were followed continuously, suspected of being agitators. It was not long, however, before they were accepted as harmless and left alone.

Madame had slipped into the habit of spending most of the day in an old red dressing gown or in voluminous kaftans to hide her bulk. After a time, however, she began to realize she had to learn to get on with the European community in India and she would dutifully slip into a black silk dress and sip sherry. Her effort brought dividends in the shape of A. P. Sinnett, then editor of *The Pioneer* in India. He and his wife were received into the Society, and they invited Madame Blavatsky and Colonel Olcott to stay with them at their house in Simla.

Sinnett was fascinated by her. 'Personally her manners were rough,' he admitted, 'but she had a lively humour and bright intelligence . . . her rugged manners and disregard of all conventionalities were the result of a deliberate rebellion against refined society.'

The headquarters of the Theosophist Society in Bombay were established at a place called Breach Candy in a bungalow perched high above the road. Madame Blavatsky worked there from morning till night, smoking like a chimney and pouring out articles which brought in money to keep them afloat. Colonel Olcott travelled all over India forming new branches. The bungalow had been empty for some years because people said it was haunted, but Madame found the atmosphere sympathetic. Streams of visitors found their way there. She would greet them warmly, then hurry off to the seclusion of an inner room where, she explained, she could prepare herself in the silence to receive whatever messages or orders were coming through from her astral masters, the Mahatmas Koot Hoomi and Morya.

In 1882 she became seriously ill with a kidney disease and suspected that what she called the term of her physical life was over. She was completely restored to health by occult teachers and healers, including a Tibetan priest. Feeling her old energy return, she declared the bungalow was too small for the growing needs of the Society. A spacious house was found at Adyar on the outskirts of Madras, which stood in extensive grounds beside a broad, shallow estuary. She declared it perfect and moved there just before Christmas. The Europeans of Bombay did not pretend to be anything but relieved.

Theosophy prospered and soon there were seventy-seven branches of the Society in India alone. Sanskrit scholars and Buddhist priests became interested, and eventually eight more branches were established in Ceylon (now Sri Lanka). Madame Blavatsky felt she had at last found the tranquil retreat where she could spend the rest of her life. She had an 'occult room' where she retired to contact the Mahatmas and take down the teachings and advice they wished to be passed on to the faithful. What became known as The Mahatma Letters became the centre of a storm of controversy. It was blasphemously suggested by some that she had written the letters herself!

This was not the only storm brewing when Madame and the Colonel left India for a visit to Europe in February 1884. A married couple called Coulomb had for some years been working as housekeeper and gardener at the Society headquarters. The arrangement turned sour. Madame Coulomb began dropping hints that she had assisted Madame Blavatsky to produce some of her phenomena, and further suggested that the Society was under the patronage of the devil. The Coulombs sold to a Christian missionary magazine a bundle of letters which, they said, had been written by the Theosophists' founder to her housekeeper. They were, if genuine, painfully incriminating.

Madame Blavatsky furiously denied having written the letters. 'Sentences here and there I recognize. They were taken from old notes of mine. But there are so many mistakes. For instance, I am not so ignorant of Indian affairs that I would refer to the Maharajah of Lahore when every Indian schoolboy knows there is no such person. . . .' She also pointed out that she had been producing phenomena without the Coulombs' assistance for most of her life.

Nevertheless, the letters created something of a *cause célèbre* in the occult world. Finally the Society for Psychical Research sent Richard Hodgson to find out what was going on. His judgment was not favourable. Not only did he judge the Coulomb letters to be genuine but he also said that Madame Blavatsky was responsible for the Mahatma Letters. She accused Hodgson of examining only her sworn enemies, and protested that she had not been allowed to see one line of the controversial correspondence. Her only solace came from students of the Colleges in Madras, who joined together to welcome her back from Europe with a loyal address which began 'Dear and revered Madame . . . you have dedicated your life to the disinterested service of occult philosophy; you have thrown a flood of light on the sacred mysteries of our hoary religion and philosophies. . . .'

The scandal ended her life in India. Such was her burning sense of injustice that she would pace up and down her room in Adyar for hours, eyes blazing, raging and cursing in Russian. Eventually the doctors said she would drop dead if she did not have peace and quiet. Towards the end of March 1885 she left for good. Sick and totally demoralized by the accusations that had been made against her, she moved first to Italy, then to Germany, where she found quiet lodgings in the town of Würzburg. She began to write her magnum opus, *The Secret Doctrine*.

Countess Wachtmeister, a Theosophy student, heard that she was ill and lonely and offered to join her as nurse and companion. 'I had been told a great deal against her and can honestly say I was prejudiced in her disfavour,' she wrote in her reminiscences. 'It was only a sense of duty and gratitude which caused me to take on the task. I had gained a lot from Theosophy. After hearing the rumours circulating about her — that she was practising black magic, fraud and deception — I was on my guard. But after a few months I was ashamed of myself for having ever suspected her. . . . I believe her to be an honest and true woman, faithful to death to her Masters and to the cause for which she has sacrificed position, fortune, health.' The Countess stayed with her till the end.

Controversy was still rumbling round Madame Blavatsky's head when, in the spring of 1891, she suffered a severe attack of influenza. She was now living in England, lecturing to her still numerous followers and working on her enormous book. She did not recover and on May

8, 1891, died in the company of three of her Theosophists, who entwined her in their arms as she quietly passed away. The turbulent Russian spirit was still. Those present said a great sense of peace filled the room. Though she was cremated at Woking half her ashes were sent to her beloved Adyar, the rest to the American Theosophical Society, where it all began.

The Maharishi

A small, giggling guru from the foothills of the Himalayas has brought about a small but significant revolution in the modern world. The Maharishi Mahesh Yogi, whose disciples included the Beatles, introduced the act of Transcendental Meditation to stress-torn America and Europe. At the height of his fame in the sixties he sold Mantras to worn-out businessmen, offered jaded show-business stars a new and deeper way to live and persuaded thousands of ordinary, everyday people that a technique based on ancient Indian philosophy could bring natural fulfilment and a new depth of creative awareness.

The Maharishi, a picturesque figure always dressed in flowing white, his long greying hair and thick beard tangling with the crystal beads round his neck, emerged as a cult figure when John, Paul, George and Ringo went to stay at his settlement at Rishikesh on the banks of the Ganges in India. The epitome of 'flower power', he became almost the father figure of the hippy era. He popped up all over the place, talking earnestly about 'bliss consciousness' one minute, giggling infectiously the next.

Transcendental Meditation is a technique which enables you to purge the mind of irrelevant and distracting thought. You achieve this by focusing the mind on a 'mantra', which is simply a word given to you individually and privately. The Maharishi says he bases his system on the *Rig Veda*, an ancient Indian science of creative intelligence.

He believes it is the answer to the stress, rigidity and routine of modern life. All that is necessary is for modern man to establish another routine by meditating for half an hour twice a day. 'You can't live without routine, it is natural to human life, so don't attempt it. Break open your rigidity instead by allowing your mind to become unbounded twice a day.'

It is known that there are now well over a million T.M. practitioners in America alone, and the Maharishi's technique is considered so successful it has been adopted by some airline companies, educational authorities, private industries and prisons. From the evidence now available some medical authorities think it can make a contribution to the treatment of stress illnesses such as hypertension, and could even be used in treating drug addicts.

Where did he begin? 'At the feet of my master,' he answers. He spent thirteen years as a young man at Kidarnath in the Himalayas learning yoga techniques from His Holiness Swami Brahmananda Saraswati Maharaj, who presided over Kidarnath, one of the four most holy places in India. He was the senior of the guru's two disciples and expected to become his successor as head of the shrine. But the younger disciple was chosen instead, The Maharishi tried to establish his claim in the courts, but failed.

He decided to start his own spiritual regeneration movement in 1958 at Rishikesh on the banks of the River Ganges. The rich and the famous as well as the devout started going to him to learn how to use the mantra properly. From time immemorial mantras have been used in the East to 'harness the mind and bring it back from erratic thought journeys'. The most famous of all is the word 'Om', which the Hindus believe to be the word of God, the primordial sound.

Within a few years the Maharishi had raised nearly one million pounds to establish an academy fit to receive overseas disciples like Shirley MacLaine, Mia Farrow, Deborah Kerr and the Beatles. John, Paul, George and Ringo abandoned their fame for a short time to be with him. John and Paul were disappointed. They had expected a saint and found he was human. George Harrison, who had been studying Indian religions ever since he learned to play the sitar, was the most dedicated of his followers and stayed longer than the other three.

The Maharishi's disciples would find him sitting cross-legged on a couch, barefoot, toying with a yellow carnation. One minute he would be the sage, the next simply a high-voiced Indian with an almost girlish sense of humour. His impact on an audience came from his total lack of selfconsciousness, combined with a hypnotic gaze from a pair of sparkling brown eyes.

He was reported to live very simply, taking only a sip of honeyed water for breakfast and simple vegetable foods in the heat of the day, yet with his rise to fame and fortune he began to display an almost childish love of luxury in other things. 'Transcendental Meditation does not reject the material world,' he pointed out, 'it merely teaches one to acquire greater happiness within it.'

From 1967 onwards his teaching thrived. He established sixty centres in various countries with tens of thousands of followers. Yellow carnation in hand, he set out on a nine-year teaching tour of the world at the end of which he said he would retire and return to the life of a solitary guru in the Himalayas. There was a distinct element of showmanship in his methods, but he obviously believed passionately in his message. The media christened him 'the jet set monk'.

He bought two old hotels set on a mountainside in Switzerland above Lake Lucerne and turned them into a headquarters for his movement in a tiny village called Seelisburg which became 'The International Capital of the Age of Enlightenment'. He would be interviewed at airports, railway stations and in hotel foyers, always conducting himself with smiling tranquillity in his perpetual rush from place to place. His Achilles' heel, much commented upon, was his love of luxury when on the move. He would stay in Hilton hotels, travel in Daimlers and set up court in railway carriages, sitting barefoot on goatskin rugs.

Accused of making a fortune out of T.M., he insisted that he himself had no money— 'I am a monk without pockets' — but that he needed big resources to build his academies. The Maharishi had indeed turned into a fund-raiser supreme, and his followers were persuaded to contribute a week's wages to his centre in India. People said they were disillusioned that he did not do more to help the poor, and noticed the fact that he had a private helicopter and three ivory Mercedes cars.

Still, he went round the world seven times and left a worldwide organization, steadily growing. 'Anyone can meditate,' he told rapt audiences. 'There are no racial or religious barriers. After it you became a more spiritually creative human being.'

Governments, he said, could solve their problems if their leaders took time off night and morning to meditate. 'If only ten per cent of the world took to constructive meditation the infectious tensions that breed war would diminish below the point of danger.' With that he disappeared into the fastnesses of the Himalayas.

Sai Baba

Satya Sai Baba, a small, chubby Hindu with a halo of black crinkly hair, is regarded by countless people as a miracle worker and a god incarnate. In India there are now 3,000 centres and five universities to promote his teachings, and books could be filled with accounts of the feats he has performed. Some of them defy belief.

He is known to have materialized out of thin air almost anything from a diamond to a deerskin. For children he will produce flowers and sweets; for the hungry, food; for his followers religious idols, books and medallions. Yet the bright red robe he wears has no pockets and only narrow wrists and no one has yet been able to explain what he does.

These so-called 'miracles' are only a small part of his extraordinary life in which he is said to have healed thousands, brought people back from the brink of death and given the impression that he has limitless knowledge and wisdom. In forty years he has risen from being a village urchin to being a potent influence on modern thought, teaching that there is 'nothing more precious within the human grasp than love'.

Sai Baba was born in India on November 23, 1926, and was a normal, robust boy who liked to run with the village children. His popularity was ensured by his strange ability to produce sweets from an empty bag. Apart from his habit of bringing home beggars for his mother to feed, he did not show any other signs of sainthood. His father thought he would make a good government officer.

Indications that he was going to be quite spectacularly different came with a dramatic incident that took place when he was thirteen. Out walking with friends, he suddenly leapt into the air with a loud cry of pain, holding his right foot. It was thought he had been stung by a scorpion. Nothing more happened to him, however, until the following evening when he suddenly fell in a swoon to the ground. When he came round he seemed to be a different person and quoted passages in Sanskrit far beyond his knowledge.

His parents thought their young 'Satya' (as he was then called) had been possessed by a demon, and called in the exorcist who nearly killed him with various gruesome treatments. The boy did not complain. Instead he sought to please his family with a demonstration of his new powers. With a wave of his hand he produced sweetmeats and flowers from nowhere. This was too much for his father. He fetched a hefty stick and faced his son. 'What are you?' he shouted. 'What are you?' and Satya replied, 'I am Sai Baba.'

His family did not know what he meant, but various educated men in the village did. The original Sai Baba was a Hindu holy man who came from Shirdi and had performed many miracles in his life. He died in 1918 but promised his followers he would come again. Many people are sceptical about this reincarnation claim, and the story of young Satya's progress to Hindu sainthood is sensational enough without it.

From producing flowers and sweets out of the air he went on to materialize holy ash. The original Sai Baba healed the sick with ash from a fire he kept constantly burning in the mosque at Shirdi. Satya Sai Baba scooped ash from the air, produced it from empty urns, and sprinkled it over his followers and visitors, even telling them to eat it to cure disease and sickness.

His psychic phenomena increased, though he regarded them as 'small items' compared with his main task of spiritual teaching. When Howard Murphet, author of *Sai Baba, man of miracles*, visited him he asked the year of his birth then, with a flick of the wrist and a wide grin procured for him a genuine newly minted American coin with his birth date stamped beneath a profile of the Statue of Liberty. Healing became an important part of his work. One of the most remarkable stories told of his healing power concerns a sixty-year-old factory owner who went to see Sai Baba at his Puttaparti headquarters in 1953. He had severe gastric ulcers which were making his life a misery. The man was given a room and left there. His condition got worse and eventually he went into a coma. Sai Baba did nothing but told the man's wife, 'Don't worry. Everything will be all right.' But instead of getting better the patient became very cold, turned blue and stiff and breathed in such a way that his wife thought she had heard the 'death rattle'. Sai Baba was quite unperturbed. He visited the room but left without saying a word. By the third day the body was almost corpse-like and his wife begged to be allowed to take it away. Sai Baba again told her to have no fear. Going into the room, he found the family weeping. He asked them to leave, and remained with the body for a few minutes. When they were called back again there was the 'dead' man sitting up in bed, smiling. The gastric ulcers were cured, never to return.

Sai Baba says he never sleeps. He has too much to do. His 'miracles' have gained him wide attention but it is his teaching that has won him an estimated 50 million devotees and outside India established fifty centres of learning in the Western world.

He claims he does not read books or meditate, he has never had a guru and was inattentive at school. But he quotes from the Bible, the Koran, Socrates, Samuel Johnson, Kant and Karl Marx, and has vast knowledge of the ancient Hindu scriptures. It is said that he has a genius for lucid exposition of the most abstruse theological conundrums and that many religious teachers have come away from an interview with him having been enlightened on problems that have perplexed them all their lives.

He teaches that 'the purpose of life is to grow in love' and says 'I have come to repair the ancient highway to God. I have not come on behalf of any sect, creed or religion. I have come to light the lamp of love in the hearts of all humanity.' But he cautions: 'Spiritual growth is slow. It should be like an oak tree rather than a Japanese larch.' Then, typically, he will put his words of wisdom into modern vernacular. 'Start early, drive slowly, arrive safely.'

His primary aim in his present incarnation, he says, is to lead the world away from violence and hatred towards compassion. To avert the nuclear holocaust. But to do that he may have to be born again. A triple incarnation to save the world from destruction was forecast in the Upanishads 5,600 years ago: if Shirdi Sai Baba was the first and Satya Sai Baba the second, he will have to be born again as Prema Sai. The chubby Hindu with his halo of hair and cherubic smile has every confidence that he will.

CHAPTER SIX

Mind over Matter

Just a few people have shown us that the mind is still
master over matter: some have demonstrated their
special abilities as automatic writers, taking down what
the 'spirit' dictates, and others have shown their
power over material things.

Geraldine Cummins

Geraldine Cummins, a tiny Irishwoman from County Cork, sat at her
desk in the 1920s and wrote a vidid, compelling addition to the New
Testament. Her words, biblical in style, continued the story of Paul,
telling how slaves tried to murder Barnabas, his companion of the
great missionary journeys, and giving an utterly convincing picture of
the political and religious turmoil of the Middle East after the death
of Christ.

She was not writing fiction. The book she published, *The Scripts of
Cleophas*, had been dictated to her, she claimed, by someone who had
lived in biblical times and knew the course of early Christian history.
The communicator — said to be an agent or messenger from the long-
dead Cleophas of the title — poured out detailed information about
the period between the death of Jesus and Paul's departure for Athens,
filling in periods that had always been considered a closed book by
religious scholars.

The scripts aroused great curiosity among churchmen. Many had
doubts about the origin of the material. Some considered she had
been sacrilegious in daring to add to Holy Scripture. But others were

impressed — especially when they found she had no knowledge of the Greek, Latin or Hebrew that would have been necessary had she obtained her material simply through research.

Geraldine Cummins was in fact considered by many in psychic circles to be the greatest automatic writer this century. She produced a staggering amount of work from 'the spirit world'. The words dictated by the messenger of Cleophas were taken down at the rate of 1,500 words an hour. She eventually had notes totalling over one million words from which she wrote her best-seller. A small audience of distinguished churchmen, scholars and psychical investigators gathered in the Bishop of Kensington's study. They clustered round watching with amazement as she took up a pencil and started to write at a tremendous speed. Pages of the Cleophas scripts were being taken down before their eyes.

Afterwards a statement was issued. Scholars and churchmen admitted there was a great deal in the scripts which 'considering the life and mentality of the intermediary, Miss Cummins, appears quite inexplicable on the supposition of human authority.' The Bishop of London's examining chaplain, Dr W. E. Oesterley, went even further. He described the scripts as being 'wonderfully evidential'.

Geraldine Cummins herself had quite different feelings about the book she produced. 'I am not proud of the Cleophas series,' she wrote. 'They are not of me. They are foreign in character to my Celtic, racial self.' She did not like St Paul anyway because of his reactionary attitude towards women. 'Why then was I compelled against my will and prejudice to write about him in such glowing terms?'

She was born in 1890 in the county of Cork, one of eleven children of the Professor of Medicine at Cork University. A precocious Spiritualist, she was introduced to the psychic world by her father's coachman at the age of five. She did nothing much about it. Her literary talent, which blossomed at an early age, took up most of her time. She was only twenty-two when one of the first plays she collaborated on was performed at Dublin's famous Abbey Theatre. She wrote short stories for London's *Pall Mall Gazette* and turned out two successful novels, all by perfectly normal means.

Her psychic development came later, after meeting Helen Dowden, a famous medium and automatic writer, in Paris in June 1914. The two women became close friends, and under Helen Dowden's guidance Geraldine began experimenting with spirit communications, then tried her hand at automatic writing. She had to work hard. At first she did not seem to have a great deal of psychic aptitude, and her attitude to her work was always that of a researcher, cool and appraising. By the mid-1920s, however, she was producing automatic scripts at an astonishing rate.

Sitting alone in a room with nothing more than a pad of notepaper and a pencil, over the years she wrote fifteen books transmitted from 'the other world'. She often produced private communications by the same method, and those they were intended for always expressed astonishment at the amount of significant and convincing detail. Some of her sitters were very famous. Canadian prime minister Mackenzie King usually tried to see her on his visits to London. She was living in a house in Chelsea, but she was often smuggled into the hotel where he was staying in order to avoid attention from the Press. Once she conducted a séance sitting on his bed while he sat propped up with pillows after a bout of 'flu. At another séance, in 1948, she acted as intermediary for the former American President Franklin D. Roosevelt, who had died in 1945. He warned the Canadian premier of a bloody and terrible war in Korea and told him of General de Gaulle's coming to power as President of France in 1958.

Geraldine Cummins was a close friend of Rosamund Lehmann, the novelist, and of the two Irish writers Violet Martin of Ross — whose pseudonym was Martin Ross — and Edith Somerville, who together wrote the immensely popular stories about the Irish R.M. Everyone thought their collaboration was at an end when Violet Martin died, but she continued to contribute, unknown to the world at large, through the hand of the medium. The publishers were forced to agree to her name appearing with Edith's on works written after her death.

But it was not until 1959, when Geraldine was sixty-nine, that she achieved the high point of her mediumship with what became known as the Cummins-Willett scripts. Eventually published in 1965 in her last book *Swan on a Black Sea* they proved to be an astonishing series of communications from a dead mother to her sceptical son.

Geraldine was on holiday in Bantry Bay in the summer of 1957 when she received a letter from W. H. Salter, honorary secretary of the Psychical Research Society. He said he thought he had a case that would interest her. A member of the SPR had lost his mother some months ago and wanted to give her the opportunity of sending him a message. Salter told Geraldine he proposed to restrict the information given to her in order to make any success she had the more striking. He only told her that the member of the SPR referred to was Major Henry Tennant. She did not know him. His mother, the late Mrs Charles Coombe Tennant, was a formidable, fascinating woman, Britain's first woman delegate to the League of Nations, a society hostess, art patron and magistrate. She had also been, unknown to most people, a skilled medium working under the name Winifred Willett.

The crucial question was, did Geraldine Cummins know her fellow-medium's true identity? She shut herself away in a quiet room and five days after being given Major Tennant's name received the first script from his mother: 'There comes to me from the earth such a feeling of depression, of worrying, of anxiety, of fear of death and all derived from non belief . . . if they could but realize half the glory, even a fragment of the peace of this life I now experience.'

She worked, alone, for two years until forty scripts had been completed by November 23, 1959. They were full of detail about names, people, places, experiences and events in the Tennant family. It emerged eventually that part of the material she had taken down was 'too correct about private affairs to be published'. Mrs Willett's sceptical son found only one incorrect name and wrote to the medium, 'The more I study these scripts, the more deeply I am impressed by them.'

As to whether Geraldine Cummins knew of the link between Mrs Willett and Mrs Coombe Tennant before she began — the question was dismissed as irrelevant in view of the mass of detail in the scripts. How could she, people asked, produce such intimate information without contact?

Geraldine Cummins regarded the scripts as the most important work of her life. According to an article in *Psychic News*, she felt she was at last provided with the irrefutable evidence she demanded to satisfy her of survival after death.

She went to find out the truth in September 1969, dying in her own County Cork. She was seventy-nine.

Rosemary Brown

One dull afternoon in 1964 Rosemary Brown, a middle-aged housewife living in a Victorian terraced house in Balham, South London, sat down at her piano to play a simple tune. She had bought the instrument second-hand, taken a few lessons and could just about manage a few hymns and popular ballads. Suddenly her hands were flying over the keys, music she had never heard before was filling the air. She had a feeling of elation, of intense pleasure in the beauty of the sound. Looking up, she saw a striking figure standing beside her. It was the virtuoso Hungarian pianist and composer Franz Liszt, who had died in 1886.

That afternoon Liszt did not say a word to her. But he returned. 'He took over my hands like a pair of gloves,' was how she described her experience. The first few visits were dream-like, though she was fully conscious. Then she began to realize she was expected to write down the music. She had had very little instruction and did not possess natural pitch, but slowly and laboriously, with the help of the composer, she conquered the technicalities. Soon her first 'master work' was on paper.

One by one, she said, they came to her — the spirits of Chopin, Beethoven, Debussy, Schumann, Bach, Rachmaninov and Brahms, Berlioz and Monteverdi — queuing up to use her as their amanuensis to communicate their unwritten works. In their own individual ways they taught her how to notate orchestral and piano works, part operas and songs. Beethoven dictated part of his tenth symphony, Chopin gave her piano sonatas and Igor Stravinsky put in an appearance fourteen months after his death in 1971 to dictate sixty lines of music.

Critics who examined the manuscripts varied in their opinions as to their artistic merit. But most agreed that in their style and content the transcriptions bore an uncanny resemblance to the composers' known works and that only an advanced musician could have written them.

That afternoon in 1964 was not the first time she saw the ghost of Franz Liszt. He first appeared to her when she was only seven years old, though she did not realize who he was until much later when she saw a photograph of him, taken in old age, in a music book. The visitation took place in an attic bedroom at the top of the big old house she lived in with her parents. She was not frightened. She was already used to seeing spirits. Snuggled down in her rickety bed, she peeped over the covers and solemnly gazed at the figure of the Abbé Liszt with his long, white hair and black cassock. He simply said, 'When you grow up I will come back and give you some music.'

During her schooldays Rosemary had flashes of telepathy and some-times visions of 'people on a different plane'. Once she saw the street she lived in as it was before any houses were built there. But otherwise she was a normal, healthy, outgoing schoolgirl. She took piano lessons for a short time, practising at home in a freezing cold 'parlour' on a piano with several dud keys, then had to give them up because her parents could not afford them. Later in her teens she managed two terms with a good music teacher by paying for lessons out of the money she earned by running errands, and there were a few other lessons. She learned the basics, but hardly attained the standard of a concert pianist.

After school she worked in the Civil Service, married and had two children, but in 1961 her husband died after a prolonged illness, leaving her penniless. Her life became a constant struggle to make ends meet, but she began to feel the comforting presence of a spirit she realized later was Liszt.

The one luxury she had allowed herself during those difficult years was an old second-hand piano. One afternoon in 1964, recuperating at home after an accident in the school kitchen where she worked, she decided to play a few pieces to pass the time. Liszt, this time in his

Rosemary Brown communicating unwritten works of great composers

dark, handsome prime, appeared vividly by her side. She found he was guiding her hands. On later visits he communicated verbally in heavily accented English. Gradually, she says, she began to look upon him as a friend. They would discuss the world and its problems and subjects like reincarnation. But his fiery temperament had obviously not been changed by his removal to another world. One day when he had made her correct a passage over and over again she became frustrated and tired and muttered that he was nothing more than an old fuss-pot. He went off in a huff and did not return for three weeks.

Liszt introduced her to Chopin. 'He looks so very young,' she wrote in her autobiography. 'He has a beautiful clear smile . . . and exquisite manners. He looks and moves like an aristocrat, but his manner seems very natural somehow, not a pose.' Chopin offered to help her with fingering. 'He tells me what the notes and chords are and then we try it out on the piano. If I'm attempting a chord and my fingers are on the wrong notes, there will be a very gentle pushing until they are correct.' Chopin, she said, had a rather husky voice, not deep, but with a strong Polish accent. He proved to be a perfect gentleman, sometimes accompanying her to concerts. One day when they were immersed in a piano sonata Chopin suddenly held up his hand to stop her and reminded her that she had left the bath-water running!

Rosemary liked Brahms. She found him both serene and strong. 'He has extraordinary patience and usually manages to communicate without difficulty, sustaining the link for long periods at a time'. She took down piano music and string quartets from him, one of which was played at the end of a BBC documentary programme. 'Because of the string quartets, I have to take much of his music down by hand,' she wrote. 'I remember the first time he arrived with the intention of giving me music. I was sitting at the piano. I played what he gave me as well as I could but it became difficult as he uses tenths a lot. My hands, unfortunately, are too small to stretch this far, though I can manage better than I used to. I think that Brahms must have had an extraordinary span between his fingers when he was alive. . . .'

Beethoven did not arrive until 1966. For a long time he remained an enigma. One of the first things she realized was that he was no longer deaf. Communication between them was slow because Rosemary was in such awe of him. 'He is an awe-inspiring person to look at and there is no doubt he was one of the greatest souls to live in this world.' At first he would impress the music upon her mind without saying a word. At those silent meetings she was overwhelmed by his greatness, but gradually began to realize that Beethoven had in fact a great simplicity, which was truly sublime. Gradually a bond of sympathy sprang up between them. She even saw something of his notorious bad temper. He cried out, 'Mein Gott!' when the doorbell rang one day when they were hard at work.

Debussy rushed in and out and sometimes disappeared for weeks, Rachmaninov was difficult at first but friendly later, Schubert tried to sing his compositions to her in a rather flat voice. She enjoyed working with Bach: 'He is able to get his ideas over to me very clearly. He must have a very methodical mind. He dislikes my working at the piano and prefers just to tell me the notes.'

In 1970 a long-playing record of some of the works was released to a mixed reception from the critics, some of them obviously extremely puzzled as to what to make of it. Hephzibah Menuhin, brilliant pianist sister of the great violinist, said, 'I look at these manuscripts with immense respect' and Leonard Bernstein, and his wife, who entertained Rosemary in their London hotel suite, were impressed both by her sincerity and by the music she showed them. Composer Richard Rodney Bennett said, 'You couldn't fake music like this without years of training. I couldn't have faked some of the Beethoven myself.'

Why the great composers should have chosen this modest, pleasant housewife to communicate their unwritten works remains a mystery. But Rosemary Brown felt the motivation was explained in a statement which 'came through' from distinguished musician Sir Donald Tovey: 'The musicians who have departed from your world are attempting to establish a precept for humanity, i.e. that physical death is a transition from one state of consciousness to another, wherein one retains one's individuality. . . .'

She had enough humour, however, to admit that she found it hard to sit and listen to some classical music. 'Poulenc visited me once or twice and tried to give me some pieces. I didn't really care for them!'

Pearl Curran

Pearl Curran was regarded as nothing more exciting than a quiet, plain-living housewife by her friends and neighbours in St Louis, Missouri. She baked well, kept a tidy home but never showed any interest in the world beyond the southern United States.

Then, one fateful evening in July 1913, she somewhat reluctantly went to a séance. What happened there turned her into a literary phenomenon, a prolific writer of novels, poetry and plays, a creator of stories told in perfect Elizabethan English and of manuscripts rich in detail of places entirely foreign to her experience. Her friends could not believe that the woman they had known for years could become the author of such a wealth of literature. And, according to her account of the extraordinary affair, they were right. She was merely passing on the work of someone long dead, and had discovered her gift as one of the world's greatest automatic writers.

That July evening at the séance she placed her hand on the ouija board and waited, hoping for a message from a relative who had recently died. She became excited when the pointer began to move, apparently struggling to spell out a name. Eventually a message became clear: 'Many moons ago I lived. Again I come . . .' and the name Patience Worth was spelled out.

Further séances produced the information that Patience Worth was a Quaker girl who had died in 1641. She had been born and raised in Dorset, in England, and had to work long, hard hours in the fields as well as helping her mother with domestic chores until her family emigrated to America as settlers. She was killed when a raiding party of Indians set fire to their homestead. She had not enjoyed her life on earth but felt unfulfilled, as though she had something more to give the world. She wanted Pearl Curran to write books for her.

At first the material came via the ouija board, letter by letter, but that soon proved too slow and clumsy. Mrs Curran then tried the usual method of automatic writing, simply holding her pen over a sheet of plain paper and letting it write of its own accord. But the speed of delivery was too fast. Finally she brought in a professional shorthand-taker so that she could simply dictate the words and sentences that went racing through her head.

The sum total of her work amounted to more than three million words of manuscript, thousands of poems and the material for six published books, a great deal of it rare and historical. It astounded academics and critics on both sides of the Atlantic.

The astounding fact about Pearl Curran is that her experience of life had been so narrow before the appearance of Patience Worth. She was not fond of reading. She had been sent to an elementary school and her education ended before she was fifteen. She admitted her knowledge of history was so sketchy that she was convinced for years that it was Henry VIII and not Charles I who had been executed by Cromwell. Poetry was not one of her favourite subjects either. She thought Tennyson's favourite poem was called *The Lady of Charlotte*. After her marriage she seldom left St Louis but concentrated her energies on being a housewife and singing in the church choir.

Mrs Curran was fascinated by what was happening to her but sometimes bewildered by Patience Worth's quaint manner of speaking and her use of old Quaker dialect. On one occasion she was advised: 'Thine own barley corn may weevil, but thee'lt crib thy neighbour's and sack his shelling.' After that Mrs Curran somewhat tartly asked Patience Worth to spare her the rustic speech. For a time she communicated in modern English but later slipped back into her old way of talking.

The speed at which the material came over was astounding — one night Mrs Curran took down twenty-two poems. The quality of the writing was high-flown, literary, some of it possessing a beauty, style and philosophical depth wholly beyond the reach of a Missouri housewife, however intelligent.

Over a span of nearly three decades Mrs Curran published a number of Patience Worth's historical novels, each one totally different in style and content. Critics lavished praise on *The Sorry Tale*, a book of 350,000 words written in two-hourly sessions. The story was that of a boy born in Bethlehem on the same night as Jesus Christ, whose life ran parallel to his and who ended as one of the thieves crucified with him on Calvary. Mrs Curran did no research for the story. The only previous knowledge she had of biblical lands was that taught by her

Sunday School teachers. Yet the details of social, domestic and political life in ancient Palestine and Rome and the customs of Greeks, Arabians and Jews are presented in a vivid and convincing manner. Some specialists said they were sure the books had been written by a scholar who had considerable knowledge of the Middle East at the time of Christ.

Another novel, *Hope Trueblood*, was a highly dramatic tale set in Victorian England, telling with considerable emotional power the story of an illegitimate child and its fight to be accepted by society. It was published in England under the name Patience Worth with no explanation of the strange circumstances surrounding it. The book was well received by both critics and public.

Another great success was her epic poem *Telka*, an idyll of medieval England containing 60,000 words and a great deal of Middle English phraseology. She had never studied the period at school even.

Research proved that both the Elizabethan prose she used and the Middle English were accurate and genuine, and perfectly suited to the idiom of the day. But how a sixteenth-century Quaker girl came to have such a knowledge of Christ's Palestine and Victoria's England is a question that has not been fully answered. Spiritualists suggested that Patience Worth came to know about it after death, 'when all things are known'.

As was to be expected, Patience and Mrs Curran were thoroughly investigated by the psychic researchers. Members of Boston SPR searched her house thoroughly for books of an estoteric nature that could have given her background material. They did not find any. Apart from the Bible and a few books of poetry with the pages uncut, the Currans did not keep an extensive library.

Mrs Curran never lost her sense of surprise that this should have happened to her. She confessed that only a few years previously she would not have been able to read her own novels with any understanding at all. She was often invited to literary receptions and there were attempts to lionize her, but she always sent her regrets. She had a feeling that for many people the mystery of who had actually written the novels was the greatest attraction.

Perhaps the strangest aspect of the whole business was something that did not concern the literary world. Patience Worth had obviously been a spinster in her short, unhappy life on earth. She conveyed to Mrs Curran a sense of frustration that she had never married and had children. One day she instructed Mrs Curran to adopt a baby girl so that they could bring it up together. Patience said the baby must have red hair, blue eyes and be of Scottish descent. She was obviously describing herself.

The Currans found a child to adopt who fitted the description perfectly and she became known as Patience Worth Wee Curran. The child grew up under the ghostly eye of Patience, who insisted on her wearing Quaker-like dresses with white collar and cuffs which made her stand out from the other girls at school. When she grew up she moved to California, where she married twice.

Mrs Curran died in 1938 and Patience Worth was never heard of again. But five years later, when she was only twenty-seven, her adopted, 'shared' daughter had a premonition of approaching death. She began to lose weight rapidly and just before Christmas 1943 died in her sleep.

So who was Patience Worth? She dictated the following poem to Mrs Curran which is all we shall ever know, for records have shown no trace of her.

A phantom? Weel enough,
Prove thee thyself to me!
I say, behold here I be,
Buskins, kirtle, cap and petty skirts,
and much tongue!
Well, what has thou to prove thee?

Coral Polge

Coral Polge would probably be considered an excellent portrait artist by any standard. Her work has one difference that makes it remarkable. When she draws in the features, hair-line and fine character details that make a face instantly recognizable she is not working from a living model. She is a psychic artist who draws her inspiration from the spirit world.

Through her thousands of people have received sketches in pencil or pastels of faces they thought they would never see again.

She has demonstrated her extraordinary artistic talent in Europe, Scandinavia, Canada, the United States and Australia. Television crews have filmed her at work, and she has been seen by large audiences at public demonstrations, projecting her drawings as they 'come through' onto an overhead screen so that every stroke of her pencil can be followed. Yet she still thinks of what she does as an intensely personal thing. Some people burst into tears when they see the outlines of a much-loved face begin to appear on a sheet of drawing paper. Others are just overcome with joy. Others are sceptical and talk about telepathy.

Her first drawings were done in graveyards. She grew up in the East End of London, where her father was a cinema manager, and as a schoolgirl had a morbid interest in death. She took to haunting churchyards, and used her emerging artistic talent to draw weeping stone angels.

The family moved to Harrow, where she attended Harrow Art School and decided to specialize in textile design. She was, she once said, fine at drawing things she could actually see, but her teachers considered her to have little imagination. 'Obviously in psychic art, imagination is a hindrance and just gets in the way, so my lack of it has proved an advantage.' Her first job on leaving art school was painting lampshades for a shop in Regent Street, then she found work as a commercial artist, drawing the illustrations for advertisements. Later she moved to a firm which specialized in retouching copies of old photographs, a job which demanded both patience and skill in dealing with fine detail.

As an attractive young woman of twenty-three, she was introduced to Spiritualism. Both her parents had visited spiritual healers at one time or another, but neither of them claimed any psychic bent. She had an aunt who read tea cups and a grandmother who might have possessed second sight, but she thought of herself as perfectly ordinary. One night, however, she went to Harrow Spiritualist Church and was singled out by a medium who asked her if she knew she had the potential to be a psychic artist. On separate occasions several other mediums asked her precisely the same thing.

With some trepidation Coral Polge took her first psychic 'circle' in 1950, just a year after her first marriage. She had no idea what would happen. To start with she found she was able to take down messages 'from the spirit world' in automatic writing. Then she found herself drawing lines, circles and meaningless shapes. Gradually faces began to appear on the paper in front of her.

To start with she tended to draw only spirit guides — solemn Red Indians and wise-looking Chinese — but as no one knew who they were, she felt her work had no point. It was when she began to draw recognizable faces that people began to get excited. One sitter watched her solemnly as she drew the features of an old man with a drooping white moustache. Suddenly she jumped up and exclaimed, 'That's my father, the living image of him!' Coral knew then she was on the right wavelength.

In the early days of her career she would usually ask the man or woman who had consulted her to give her a letter or something that had belonged to the dead person, but in time she realized it was better for her just to sit and wait until the drawing came through.

She does not, she says, see the person she is about to draw, nor is her hand controlled by psychic forces. When 'linking up' she feels a complete change of personality taking place within her. 'Having become that person, I attempt to portray his or her personality'. She 'feels' the person coming through. What appears first on the paper is an expression — a laugh or a scowl, a look of gentleness or of strength. Actual features follow after she has caught the personality.

The sketches are produced in a matter of minutes because, as she told the *Psychic News*, 'I know exactly what to draw without thinking about it. It's involuntary, like breathing or walking.' Remarkable likenesses appear on the paper of people she has never seen or known. Not only are their features usually instantly recognizable to those who love them but the psychic often portrays them in the sort of clothes they favoured when they were alive.

She married Arthur Polge in 1949, but became so engrossed in her psychic work that the marriage broke up after eight years. Faced with the necessity of earning her own living, she turned to full-time mediumship. Her second marriage was to Tom Johansen, secretary of the Spiritualist Association of Great Britain.

At the last count in 1984 Coral Polge was estimated to have produced in the region of 90,000 spirit drawings, which must make her the most prolific portrait artist of modern times.

Uri Geller

The night Uri Geller went on British television and by sheer concentration quietly proceeded to bend a variety of metal objects including forks, spoons and keys, caused a rumpus in the scientific world and an excitement among the millions who watched that has never quite died down again.

Handsome, dark-haired and only 26 years old, the Israeli entertainer seemed to demonstrate remarkable power over material things. Unable to explain what happened, he suggested, 'Perhaps everybody has got this ability within them, but it requires a certain power to trigger it off. I am sure the power must come from an intelligent form of energy.'

That evening on television, November 23, 1973, was not an exceptional one as far as Geller was concerned. He had been doing this sort of thing on stage in Israel and had achieved a certain fame as a glamorous young magician. But he was nervously aware of the immense audience watching him.

Viewers stared with amazement as David Dimbleby held a fork in his hand and it bent like wilting rhubarb as Geller stroked it with his finger. Suddenly the whole studio seemed to go haywire. A fork lying on a table bent without him even touching it, another contorted till it broke in half. Broken watches scattered in front of him began to tick but the hands inside a perfectly good watch suddenly curled up against the glass face. At the end of the programme the switchboard was jammed with viewers reporting that their own cutlery had begun to curl up as they ate TV suppers in front of the screen!

The excitement in Britain was reported all round the world. Some people posed the question if he could do that to one piece of metal was it safe to let him travel in a complicated piece of machinery like a jumbo jet. Controversy arrived with his fame and from then on he was either being treated like a pop star or accused of being a fraud. Only when he was subjected to controlled tests did the attitude change towards him. Scientists at the Max Planck Institute in Germany described his powers as 'a phenomenon which in theoretical terms cannot be explained'.

Uri Geller was born in Tel Aviv in 1946 and remembers 'strange energy forces' going back to the age of three. His family on his father's side was very religious, his grandfather having been a Rabbi in Budapest. On his mother's side he was distantly related to Sigmund Freud. When he started going to school he was given a watch which always seemed to be going wrong. Sometimes as he looked at it the minute hand would spin four or five hours ahead. Finally, he left the watch at home. His mother checked it every day but nothing unusual happened. He decided to try wearing it again, but when he glanced down in the middle of a lesson he saw the hands whirring round. When he was eating soup in the kitchen at home one day his spoon bent until the bowl fell off, and he was left holding the handle. Another time, when he was in a restaurant with his parents, forks and spoons on a near-by table began to curl up. Bewildered at first by these phenomena, he soon began to suspect that something in himself was causing them. By the age of thirteen he had gained some control over his powers.

For a time, after his parents divorced, he went to live in a kibbutz and was so unhappy there that his curious ability disappeared. There was not much time to think of it either during the 1967 war, when he trained as a paratrooper in the Israeli army and was injured by an Arab sniper. While recuperating he took a job as instructor at a children's camp about an hour's drive out of Tel Aviv. Sometimes he amused them by showing a few of the experiments he now practised in telepathy and metal-bending. They were mesmerized.

Tales of his magic spread, and by 1968 he was in demand at schools and private parties all over Tel Aviv. By the summer of 1971 he had turned himself into a brilliant entertainer who bent cutlery, broke metal rings and mended broken watches in front of huge audiences. Teenagers went wild about him. Stories about him reached the famous psychical researcher Dr Andrija Puharich, who decided it was worth flying from New York to Israel to see him. As he watched Geller perform in a discothèque in Jaffa his first impression was that Uri was no more than a skilful magician, but when he snapped a woman's dress ring in two by simply placing his hand over it as it was gripped in her fist, he began to have second thoughts.

Puharich asked Geller if he would submit to scientific tests. As he watched the Israeli raised the temperature on a thermometer by staring at it, moved a compass needle by concentration and bent a jet of water streaming from a tap by simply moving his finger towards it. Puharich flew back to America convinced that Geller was a genuine psychic with a definite power of mind over matter. He had promised he would go to New York at the earliest opportunity to demonstrate under controlled conditions.

First, Uri went to Germany. Arriving in Munich in June 1972, he was met by a crowd of reporters who asked him to do something 'really astounding'. He asked them to suggest something. 'How about stopping a cable car in mid-air?' Geller hesitated, then agreed to try. Reporters took him to the Hochfelln Funicular Line outside Munich. After two or three abortive attempts the car stopped in mid-air over a 140-metre drop. The mechanic called the control centre and was told that the main switch had flicked off of its own accord!

In America the Israeli found tough audiences, traditionally sceptical about miracle workers, and he was both tense and miserable. Most of the time, however, he was surrounded by scientists who were eager to test him. He met Wernher von Braun, famous inventor of the V-2 rocket, and impressed the great man by two incidents that took place in his office. Taking a gold ring off his finger, von Braun placed it on the palm of his hand and watched it become quite flat as Geller passed his hand over it. The scientist then found that his calculator battery was flat though he had only put it in that morning. Geller held it between his hands then passed it back to him in working condition. The delighted von Braun concluded that Geller was capable of producing strange electric currents.

Scientists at the Stanford Research Institute in California which carries out important research work for the US Government, took a film of Geller performing his feats and tested his powers of extrasensory perception. He was asked to pick out from ten small metal cylinders the one that contained a metal ball. After a few seconds concentration he went straight to the right cylinder. He succeeded in a similar test involving a cylinder of water. Geller was not always satisfied with his performance in scientific laboratories and said he was at his best before 'sympathetic audiences, small friendly gatherings of interested people'. He felt he needed the energy of others to generate his mental forces.

Soon after his triumph on British television in 1973 he set off to demonstrate his powers in Paris, Scandinavia, Spain, Italy and Japan, receiving superstar attention all the way. He returned to America, where he came under terrific pressure from his detractors, then moved on to Mexico, where he was a frequent guest at the home of the President. At the height of his fame in 1974 he wrote his autobiography and planned to star in a film about his own life. He even tried dowsing for metals from an aeroplane, and had considerable success working for gold and copper mines.

Still stealing headlines in 1984, the *New York Times* printed a report that Uri Geller had had secret talks with the former US President, Jimmy Carter, who ordered the Central Intelligence Agency to conduct a high-level review of supernormal research behind the Iron Curtain. The metal-bender warned that the Russians were studying psychic phenomena much more seriously than the Western world.

Happily married, looking handsome and fit, Geller announced in 1985 that he was planning to settle in England but he also intended to build a health centre in Israel and a laboratory for psychic research —after having worked with scientists in nearly every major country in the world.

Uri Geller tries his blindfold driving experiment

CHAPTER SEVEN
Psychic Detectives

Police forces in many countries now accept the help of psychic detectives when a case proves too hard to crack. On the Continent especially their abilities are valued. By strange coincidence two of the greatest psychic detectives of recent years have both been Dutchmen.

Robert James Lees

Was Victorian psychic Robert James Lees responsible for tracking down Jack the Ripper? There are authorities who believe he was, and that the results of his investigations lie in a black japanned box somewhere in the archives of the British Home Office.

Robert Lees was a remarkable clairvoyant who enjoyed royal patronage and was received more than once both at Balmoral and Buckingham Palace by Queen Victoria herself. His powers developed when he was very young. He was only nineteen when the Queen summoned him for the first time and discussed psychic matters with him at great length.

During the late summer and autumn of 1888, when the monster known as Jack the Ripper killed and mutilated five prostitutes in such an appalling way that a wave of terror swept over the whole East End of London, Robert Lees began to have visions. The police, desperate for clues, suspecting they were up against a sadistic madman, listened to him at first with incredulity. When his psychic detection finally led them to the 'Ripper', the information he put at their disposal being investigated, confirmed and acted upon, he was sworn to secrecy. So too were all the doctors, police and detectives who had been involved.

'Speculation has always been rife as to Jack the Ripper's identity', wrote Edwin T. Woodhull, ex-Scotland Yard man, in his account of Robert Lee's involvement in the case.

'He was never brought to justice but it is a mistake to think that the police did not know who he was. It was proved beyond doubt that he was a physician of the highest standing who lived in a fine house in the West End of London. To most people he was the most refined and gentle of men, both courteous and kind. But he was also an ardent vivisectionist and a cruel sadist who took a fierce delight in inflicting pain on helpless creatures.'

How Robert Lees became involved in the Ripper case is recounted in an early published version of his life.

One day, sitting in his study, he found himself drifting into a sort of trance and a scene began to form itself in front of him. He saw two people, a man and a woman, walking down the length of 'a mean street'. He saw them enter a kind of courtyard. They passed a public house, and by the light of a big clock he could see the hands stood at 12.30 — the time, at this period, when public houses closed.

The woman appeared to be drunk as she bumped into the man from time to time in the gas-lit alley. Judging by his walk, her companion was perfectly sober. Presently they turned into a dark place with an open door, and Lees could read the name quite clearly. It was 'George Yard Buildings'.

They leaned against the wall. Robert Lees could see that the man was dressed in a light tweed suit, and that a black felt hat was pulled well down over his eyes. Over his arm he carried a dark overcoat or mackintosh. Suddenly he put his hand over the woman's mouth, drew a knife from his pocket and slit her throat. Blood streamed over his clothes. As the woman sank to the ground he bent over her and proceeded to cut and mutilate her with the knife. This done he dragged her body into the darkness of an open doorway, slipped on the dark overcoat, fastening it up to the neck to hide any traces of blood, and slipped away.

The vision, which left Robert Lees considerably shaken, took place on the day following August Bank Holiday in 1888. The psychic was even more horrified when he realized he had witnessed the first of the 'Ripper' murders, for the papers carried a full account of what happened to Martha Turner, found with her throat cut, in the dark doorway of a common lodging house in George Yard Buildings, Commercial Street, Spitalfields.

At Scotland Yard the psychic was listened to politely but with obvious scepticism. It was only after the inquest that notice was taken of his psychic evidence and even then the police did not trouble to get in touch with him. Giving evidence, a woman friend of the dead Martha

Turner said she saw her at about 12.20 am walking in the company of a 'toff' who wore a light suit and carried a coat on his arm.

Robert Lees could not sleep for nights after his vision of the murder. His nerves were so badly affected by what he had seen that his doctor ordered him to take a holiday abroad. The psychic took his advice and went with his family to the Continent.

By the time he returned, fully recovered, two more murders had been committed, obviously by the same hand. The psychic had not been troubled by further visions, and tried to keep himself from thinking about the grisly affair.

One day, soon after the third murder, he caught an omnibus in Shepherd's Bush with his wife and began to experience the strange sensations which had preceded his first disturbing experience. At Notting Hill a man got on the omnibus and Robert Lees felt a numb, powerless sensation overtake him. As he looked up and met the man's gaze, he went icy cold. The new passenger was wearing a light tweed suit, a dark felt hat and carried a dark overcoat. 'The omnibus jogged and rumbled along until it came to Lancaster Gate, while Mr Lees was subject to every unknown feeling ever experienced by mortal man.'

At Marble Arch the man got off and Robert Lees, leaving his wife with a hasty word that he would follow her home later, also got off and began to follow him across Hyde Park. He lost him when he hailed a cab outside Apsley House. His frantic efforts to try to get a policeman to arrest him were in vain, but a police sergeant made a note of the incident.

That night he had a premonition that the Ripper was about to commit another murder. The scene was not as distinct as in his first vision but he saw clearly the terrified face of the victim. This time the clairvoyant went straight to police headquarters and demanded to see the detective in charge of the Ripper investigations. His revelations were by now so startling that it was decided to ask him to help in tracking down the sadistic monster. Accompanied by the chief detective and a number of police officers, he went to the scene of the Ripper's last murder and suffered mental agony as he 'saw' the scene re-enacted. When his clairvoyant vision ended he turned away and started to walk swiftly in a westerly direction. He had picked up the psychic trail.

Mile after mile police and detectives followed him until he reached a street in the West End of London and stood before a magnificent house. There was a terrible feeling of disappointment. This was the home of an eminent physician whose life and talents had been dedicated to the relief of suffering. But Robert Lees insisted this was where Jack the Ripper lived. Only when the psychic proved his clairvoyant powers still further by describing to them exactly what the house looked like inside, were they prepared to take a chance.

Under the most delicate questioning, the doctor's wife broke down, told how she had discovered a short time after their marriage that he had a mania for inflicting pain, how he had once nearly killed their four-year-old child and how quickly he could revert to his other self. It was a true Jekyll and Hyde story.

According to Edwin Woodhull, the doctor was declared insane and placed in a private asylum. To account for his disappearance from society it was announced that he had died suddenly from heart failure, and funeral rites were actually conducted. For his work in tracking the Ripper, Robert Lees received a life pension from the Privy Purse and was sworn to secrecy.

Peter Hurkos

Dutch detective Peter Hurkos has been connected with some of the most famous murder and missing person cases to hit the world head-lines in the last few decades. He is not attached to any police force. Only a handful of police chiefs will even admit they have consulted him. He works alone with only one weapon — his gift of psychic sight.

Hurkos has been involved with cases as infamous as the Sharon Tate murders committed by the devilish Charles Manson 'family', the tracking down of the Boston Strangler and the mysterious disappear-ance of America's Judge Chillingworth. In England he put his psychic power at the disposal of Scotland Yard when the Stone of Scone disappeared from Westminster Abbey, and in Holland he helped police capture an arsonist who turned out to be the son of a rich and respected family.

Some people in the world of psychical research refuse to take the big dark-haired Dutchman seriously, perhaps because after settling in the United States in 1958 he was taken up by the smart Hollywood set, many stars going to him for paranormal readings. Marlon Brando was reported to be fascinated, and Glenn Ford expressed an ambition to play him on screen. Hurkos basked in the bright lights. After all, before he fell off a ladder and the psychic gift came to him, he was only a run-of-the-mill house painter!

As he writes in his autobiography *Psychic*, he was born Pieter van der Hurk on May 21, 1911, in the small industrial town of Dordrecht, not far from The Hague in Holland. He adopted the name Peter Hurkos when he was in the Dutch resistance during the war. His

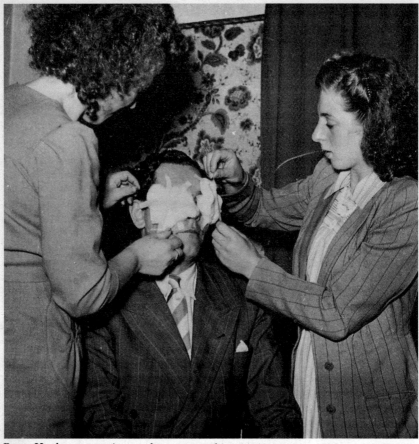

Peter Hurkos preparing to demonstrate his unique powers

father, a house-painter, did not make a lot of money but his mother was a typical meticulous Dutch housewife and he had a normal and happy upbringing. His only regret was that he had to abandon a high school course in radio engineering for lack of funds. About one thing he is certain. 'There was absolutely no history of extra-sensory perception, telepathy or any other psychic awareness within my family.'

He went to sea, first as a ship's cook, then as a stoker, finally taking a job in Shanghai as a talleyman. When the outbreak of war put an end to the Shanghai trade he returned home, married and agreed to join his father in his small business as a painter and decorator.

On a gloomy, misty day in June 1941, he was painting a four-storey building in The Hague with his father. He had agreed to tackle the high places, and to save time placed his ladder between two windows, calculating that with a bit of stretching he could paint both at once without having to climb down. But reaching for a pot of paint he lost his balance and fell. He remembers still how long it seemed to take, and how his whole life spun before him.

When he woke up in hospital he could not at first remember names, faces or dates. For a while he could not recognize members of his family. He had been unconscious for four days, suffering from concussion and severe neurological damage. He would undoubtedly have been killed but for the fact that he hit the ground shoulder first.

Something else had happened. He told his biographer, Norma Lee Browning: 'When I woke up I had no mind of my own. I was in somebody else's mind and I was scared . . . my father and mother said it's not the same Peter any more . . . they said I had died and come back with two minds. It's God's truth, I came back with two minds.' He also came back with the gift of psychic sight.

One day a stranger stopped by his bed to wish him a speedy recovery. The instant they shook hands and said goodbye Peter knew he was a British agent and that he was going to be killed by the Germans a few days later. Shocked by what was going through his mind, Peter gripped the man's arm and tried to stop him. Nurses rushed in with sedatives to calm him down. Two days later the man's death was in the newspapers.

Before Peter was discharged from hospital the doctor told him there was a possibility that the fall had damaged certain functions of the brain and stimulated others. He soon found out what the doctor meant. As the days went by he began to have more and more flashing glimpses of the past and of the future. Sometimes he was able to describe places he had never been to.

Carrying forged papers with his new name, Hurkos, he worked for the resistance in Holland during the war. Captured and sent to Buchenwald concentration camp, he nearly died from starvation and beri-beri. On his release he was decorated by Queen Juliana.

He had lost his head for heights, so was not able to take up his old job as a house-painter. Somehow, he decided, he would use his new ability to earn money. He agreed to do a number of stage performances based on psychometry (asking a member of the audience for a personal possession, he would then attempt to 'read' their lives). He was a theatrical success but turned down an offer to tour Europe, feeling there was something more important he could do with his gift. Just one incident started his career as a psychic detective.

One morning, about 3 a.m., he was wakened by the ringing of the doorbell. He answered it to find a distraught woman on the doorstep. She begged him to help her. Her husband had disappeared. The police had not been able to find him but had told her not to worry, that he was probably out with some friends. She felt sure something was wrong, and offered Hurkos any amount of money if he could find him.

The psychic asked for some object that had belonged to her husband and immediately 'saw' a football and a uniform. The man, it turned out had been a famous footballer, but was now in the army. Hurkos found the words rushing out: 'I am sorry to tell you, madame, he has fallen into an ice trap . . . he decided to take a short cut through the woods . . . he fell into a ditch — no, it is a tank trap and it is filled with water . . . he struggles, but he is too weak . . . he has drunk bad booze . . . he freezes to death in the water . . . I am sorry, madame,' 'he told her gently. 'Your husband is dead. I am very sorry.'

Hurkos made a sketch for her to take to the police station showing where they would find the body, but the police laughed at her story. She insisted they took her to the place he had described. They found nothing. Furious by what they considered was a waste of time, they warned her not to listen to Hurkos. He was a fake. Next day the woman persuaded Peter to go with her to the police. After listening to him they agreed to return to Maljebaan in The Hague, where he had 'seen' the body. This time they found the missing man's cap in the bushes. After seven days of digging they brought up the body.

The story spread like wildfire. His reputation as a psychic detective was soon established as he worked on many cases of missing people and on murders. But he soon discovered something he had to learn to live with all his career: the police did not like to admit that a psychic had helped them in their investigations.

He left Holland to work in Belgium, where he set up his head-quarters at an Antwerp hotel, sometimes giving public readings but also working on cases. When the body of George Cornelis, a former hero of the Belgian underground, was found in the River Leie a verdict of 'death by misadventure—manner unknown' was brought in by the Ghent police. But when the Cornelis family asked Hurkos to investigate, he declared, after handling his picture, that he had been killed by a monkey wrench and thrown into the river. Working with the police, he eventually tracked down two men who had been Nazi collaborators during the war and were afterwards jailed as a result of the testimony of Cornelis. They confessed to beating him to death with a wrench and throwing his body into the river. The case brought him a considerable amount of publicity since the crime had not only been solved but actually discovered through the use of extrasensory perception.

Hurkos was spending Christmas 1950 with his family and his wife, Maria, at home in Holland when he heard that the legendary Stone of Scone had been stolen from Westminster Abbey in England. The Stone, upon which Scottish kings were once crowned, had been brought to England by Edward I. For 664 years it had been safely stowed away beneath the Coronation Chair in the Abbey. Now it had gone, and England was in an uproar.

Hurkos offered his services to Scotland Yard. While they met him in some style with a police escort at London Airport, and granted him access to the Abbey, he could see from the beginning that they were embarrassed about being helped by a clairvoyant.

Walking up to the Coronation Chair, he knelt down, touched it and felt its vibrations. Pictures began to flash through his mind. He 'saw' much of the history connected with the Stone but tried to concentrate upon the theft. After about thirty minutes of intense effort — during which he seemed to be in a semi-trance state and was perspiring heavily — he began to talk: 'I see five people were involved . . . three breaking in . . . two waiting outside in a truck . . . I see an old church by a river. . . .' On he went.

The next morning he was given a crowbar that had been used to break into the Abbey, a watch-strap found near the Chair and the plaque from the Stone. Standing in Tufton Street, where the plaque had been found, it was clear to him that it had been thrown from a vehicle and that the Stone had merely passed this site on its way to another destination. Exploring the Lower Thames Street area, he found the shop where the crowbar had been bought. By the end of the day he told the men from the Yard that the thieves were in Glasgow. They had taken the Stone there, and now it was hidden in an old church. He described the five men involved in the theft and said it was a student prank. He predicted the Stone would be back in the Abbey within four weeks.

Though he drove up to Scotland he did not find anything. He went home depressed by the 'cold and unbelieving attitude' of the police, and the ridicule of the British Press. But, just as he had predicted, the Stone was found in the ruins of an old church — Arbroath Abbey in Angus. It was returned four weeks later and the thieves were traced to Glasgow.

In the rest of Europe he was gaining recognition. He never claimed to be right every time, but the percentage of his correct predictions was incredibly high. After putting him through a gruelling test, the French police used his services for the next five years. He still gave private readings and used his gift for entertainment purposes in order to pay his bills. He seldom received a fee for police work.

Stories about him appeared in *Paris Match* magazine and were seen by Dr Andrija Puharich, who was working on psychical research at the Round Table Foundation Laboratories in Maine. He invited Hurkos to go to him for six months so that he could explore his psychic powers. The Dutchman was only too willing. He still did not understand quite what had happened to him when he fell off that ladder, and hoped to learn something about himself. He performed well in the laboratory under controlled conditions and the experiments went on for two and a half years. He soon became a regular crime consultant in America, and drifted towards the rich and famous in Hollywood.

One of the most sensational cases he worked on was that of the Boston Strangler early in 1964. He only carried on his investigations for six days but lost 15 lb in weight and took months to get over the experience. The mental punishment he suffered was largely because he steadfastly refused to believe that Albert DeSalvo was the Strangler. Norma Lee Browning, the *Chicago Tribune* columnist who wrote his biography after knowing him for years, devotes a large chunk of her book to his dilemma over the Strangler.

Hurkos was staying with Glenn Ford at his home in Beverly Hills when Assistant Attorney General John S. Bottomly — who was in charge of the whole operation — called and asked him to help. The Strangler had just finished with his eleventh victim, nineteen-year-old Mary Sullivan, and there had been a public outcry. 'I didn't want to take the case,' Peter Hurkos admitted. 'I didn't like the idea of going to Boston. I knew something was wrong on that case. I didn't want to go.' But Bottomly had set up a special Strangler Investigation Bureau and promised him every assistance.

On the first day Hurkos asked for a city map and requested that it should be laid upside down so that he could not see the streets. Then he asked for an object from one of the victims. Someone produced a small comb. With the teeth of the comb he began to trace the upside-down map of Boston. He moved the comb back and forth, up and down until it stopped in the Newton-Boston area. 'Here you will find the killer,' he said suddenly. 'He looks like a priest, dresses like a priest, but he is thrown out by the monks. He speaks French. He talks like a girl — like this' — and his voice rose to falsetto. 'He's a pervert.' Next day the detectives handed Hurkos a letter which had been sent to the nursing director at Boston College School of Nursing from an address in the area that Peter had indicated on the map. Instead of reading it he crumpled it in his hand, closed his eyes and concentrated. Suddenly he cried, 'This is the one . . . the murderer . . . son of a bitch, he do it.' The writer of the letter had asked to be put in touch with a good Catholic nurse. He had given his own doctor's name so that he could be checked up on. When the doctor was contacted he said the writer of the letter was a man in his fifties with a record of mental illness. He had a problem. His brother had tried once to get him committed.

Hurkos came up with a description of the man: 'He is not too big, high hairline with a mark or spot on his left arm, something wrong with his thumb. He has a French accent . . . he has to do with a hospital . . . he is a homo and a woman-hater . . . blue-grey eyes, a killer's eyes . . . his hair is thin, he has a sharp, pointed, spitzy nose and a big Adam's apple.'

Much of what Peter Hurkos revealed about the man burst out while he was in a restless sleep. Detectives kept watch by his bed as he tossed and turned, his voice alternating between his own heavy Dutch accent and a falsetto.

He said the man lived near a seminary where priests lived. He had once tried living in a monastic order, but he was a pervert and his religion had turned sour. He thought that by killing women he was offering to God clean, female sacrifice.

In his sleep Hurkos also saw that the man slept in a room 'like a junk pile' on a bed without a mattress, and the place was full of boxes of women's shoes that he sold from door to door.

Police investigated all he had told them about the writer of the letter and the details fell into place. He went with a group of detectives to call on the man. When the door opened and a high-pitched voice asked what they wanted, Peter Hurkos turned grey-white and started to perspire. He was looking at the face he had seen in his sleep.

They had every reason to think that they had at last got the Boston Strangler, but before any move could be made the doctor questioned him at length. He admitted he had once tried to get himself committed. The doctor signed committal papers and O'Brien was on his way to Massachusetts Mental Health Centre. There was no way he could be brought to trial.

Hurkos, worn out and swearing he would never work on another murder case, flew to New York.

DeSalvo was picked up a month after he left and while waiting trial on a charge of rape and breaking and entering suddenly confessed he was the Strangler. He was committed, and Hurkos believes the two men were in the same room together at the state mental institution, and that is how DeSalvo knew exactly what to confess. DeSalvo admitted he got a kick out of the publicity the Strangler received. Hurkos pointed out that while DeSalvo was an oversexed brute where women were concerned, his appetites were normal. The killer was a pervert who displayed his victims in gross and degrading positions, indicating a woman-hater. Four years later the Strangler case was reopened and just as suddenly closed again.

Another case that cost Hurkos a great deal emotionally was the terrible massacre of Sharon Tate and four other people by the Charles Manson 'hippy' family in the late sixties. He was brought into the case by a lawyer called Peter Knecht, who had been a personal friend of one of the victims, Hollywood hairdresser Jay Sebring. The beautiful, 26-year-old film actress Sharon Tate, eight months pregnant when she was butchered and mutilated, was the wife of brilliant film director Roman Polanski. Hurkos spent weeks telling the police what he 'saw', right down to describing 'a bearded guy named Charlie'. It was his first Hollywood case, and when it was all over he swore it would be his last.

Since then Hurkos has given a great deal of his time to being tested for telepathy, clairvoyance and extrasensory perception and established a foundation of his own to make systematic studies of psychic phenomena. For in spite of all he has witnessed as a psychic detective, he says, 'I believe the growing knowledge of psychic ability has given a glimpse into a new creative dimension of human nature, giving renewed hope and determination to mankind.'

Gerard Croiset

When Pat McAdam, a Scottish teenager, went missing after hitching a lift the day after a late-night party in Glasgow on February 19, 1967, Gerard Croiset, hundreds of miles away in Holland, had a clairvoyant vision of the place where she probably met her end.

The girl's body was never found, her fate never established, but so accurate was Croiset's description that investigators were able to go straight to the location he described. He was listened to with respect because for many years he had been regarded as one of the world's foremost psychic detectives.

Seventeen-year-old Pat and her friend, Hazel Campbell, were picked up on the London Road in the outskirts of Glasgow. The lorry driver told them he was going south to Hull and could drop them somewhere close to where they lived. Pat McAdam chatted to him while her friend dozed. They stopped for a meal in a transport café. They found him very friendly, and when he swung off the main road realized he was going to make a detour and take them all the way home. Hazel was dropped off in the centre of Annan. She waved goodbye, presuming Pat would be dropped in Dumfries. But the girl never reached home. She was never seen again.

The lorry driver was tracked down after a three-week search by police, and swore he had dropped Pat McAdam on the outskirts of Dumfries and that was the last he knew of her. An intensive police hunt was set up, but to no avail.

Three years later Frank Ryan, a Dumfries journalist who had been on the case from the beginning, happened to be in Holland and decided to contact Croiset. He showed the psychic a police poster with a picture of the missing girl. Croiset stared at it for a long time, then said he saw a place where there were fir trees and exposed tree roots on the banks of a river. Near there, he said, was a flat bridge over the river with grey tubular railings. It was at the foot of a hill in an area north of Annan. Across the bridge was a cottage with advertising signs on the side of it and a white paling fence. Croiset did a drawing on a large sheet of paper and handed it to Ryan. The journalist took it back to Scotland and with a colleague went out to look at the place.

Croiset seemed to have been describing the Williamnath Bridge near the village of Dalton, where the police search had been intense. Locals had reported seeing a huge articulated lorry near there, similar to the one that had picked up the girls. But the setting was nothing like that drawn by the Dutchman. They drove on, and coming to Middleshaw on the edge of the Birkshaw forest went cold with shock. There was the scene exactly as Croiset had seen it sitting at his desk in Utrecht.

The psychic asked for something that had belonged to the missing girl and Ryan borrowed her Bible. As Croiset took it in his hand he said sadly, 'She is dead,' and went on to insist that she was buried or concealed in the area he had 'seen', in a tangle of roots on the river bank. Asked if he could give more details, he concentrated on a detailed map, then talked of a building called 'Broom Cottage,' where he said they would find a wreck of a car with a wheelbarrow propped against it.

The bridge in Croiset's first vision crossed the river called the Water of Milk west of Middleshaw and the car in the second vision was, he said, just a little farther downstream. He mentioned it only to pinpoint the area more accurately. When Ryan and a small group of friends set out to find the cottage they had no difficulty. But how in heaven's name, they wondered, could Croiset have known there was an old, broken-down Ford with a wheelbarrow propped against its back end in this exact spot when he had never even been to Scotland!

The Dutchman said he had a mental image of Pat McAdam taking her last walk with a man by the side of the river, where some trees had been felled. Later he elaborated on this, saying she had been battered to death with a heavy spanner.

Croiset eventually flew to Scotland, visited the places he had previously seen only through clairvoyance and stated he was now thoroughly convinced that her body had been thrown into the Water of Milk, caught for a while in tangled tree-roots, then carried out to sea. The river, which ran into the Solway Firth, was prone to flash floods.

Pat McAdam's fate was never finally established, but ten years later the lorry driver, Thomas Young, was arrested on charges of murder and rape in quite another connection and sent to prison for life. He boasted of having had sex with more than two hundred women in the cab of his lorry.

Hundreds of cases were investigated by Croiset and kept on file at Utrecht University. In this country he was also involved in the hunt for Mrs Muriel McKay, wife of a top Fleet Street newspaperman, kidnapped in 1969. Relatives who had heard of his work called him in. Though he managed to tell them that she had been kept for a time somewhere in a hut on the Hackney Marshes, she was never found.

Croiset was a striking figure with craggy features and a wild mop of hair. Born in 1909, the son of an actor, he had a miserable childhood, mostly in the care of foster parents. His paranormal abilities began to emerge when he was only six. He told one of his teachers that he knew he had been away for the day in order to see a blonde girl who wore a red rose. The schoolmaster had, it was true, taken leave so that he could propose to his girlfriend. Croiset's adult life was just as restless as his childhood until he married at the age of twenty-five and set up a grocery store with money given to him by his in-laws. Unfortunately, like many sensitives, he was not a good businessman, and the failure of this enterprise led him to a nervous breakdown.

There were constant reminders of his psychic ability. Once when he was talking to a watchmaker he picked up a ruler the man had been measuring with, and images of his childhood came flooding into his mind. 'You are clairvoyant,' the watchmaker told him. Croiset had a clear presentiment of the Second World War years before it was declared. He was imprisoned by the Germans, first because his mother had been a Jewess, then because he was caught working for the Dutch resistance, like Peter Hurkos.

It was not until he was thirty-six that Gerard Croiset's extraordinary powers were used to give his life meaning and direction. One night he attended a lecture on parapsychology at an adult education class in his home town of Enschede. The lecturer, who impressed him deeply, was Professor Willem Tenhaeff of Utrecht University. Something impelled him to approach the Professor when he had finished speaking. Within minutes Dr Tenhaeff realized Croiset was someone out of the ordinary and asked that he visit him at his parapsychology laboratory at the University.

Croiset offered himself for investigation, and a collaboration began between the two men that made Croiset the most celebrated clairvoyant in Europe. Tanhaeff had forty-seven other psychics and sensitives with whom he carried out scientific experiments, but Croiset was undoubtedly the star turn.

He began to work with the police, for, as Colin Wilson points out in his book *The Psychic Detectives*, in Holland the attitude of the police towards psychics is altogether less prejudiced than in England or the United States. Dutch detectives often approached the Professor to see if any of his clairvoyants could provide clues in difficult cases. Since Croiset was his star subject, he was also looked upon as Holland's chief psychic detective.

By now the father of five, Croiset was especially sensitive when it came to cases of missing children. He was asked to help police in half a dozen countries in their search for both adults and children who had disappeared. He found that in cases of accidental disappearance, when no criminal was involved, he had an eighty per cent success rate. When it came to murder, however, he admitted he often could not pinpoint the killer, but he was able to give valuable clues through clairvoyance and, as in the case of Pat McAdam, set up the scene of the crime.

One instance which demonstrated how his psychic powers could work over immense distances was recorded in December 1959. Professor Walter E. Sandelius, head of the department of Political Sciences at Kansas University in the USA, was desperate with worry about his 24-year-old daughter, Carol. She had disappeared from a hospital in Kansas where she was receiving treatment, and had been missing for eight weeks. Dr Sandelius had read about Croiset, and telephoned Professor Tenhaeff in Utrecht. He was willing, he said, to do or pay anything to find her. Tenhaeff promised that Croiset would talk to him on the phone next day.

Sitting in an office at the University, Croiset told the Kansas professor, thousands of miles away, 'I see your daughter running over a large lawn and then crossing a viaduct. Now I see her at a place where there are stores and near them a large body of water with landing stages and many small boats. I see her riding there in a lorry and in a big red car. . . .' Sandelius interrupted, 'Yes, but is she alive?' and Croiset replied, 'Yes, yes she is alive. Don't worry. You will hear something definite within six days.' On the sixth day, as arranged, Professor Sandelius went downstairs at eight o'clock in the morning to put a phone call through to Utrecht. He glanced towards the sitting room and was astounded to see his daughter, sitting on a sofa. Later she was able to confirm that the Dutch detective had seen her movements with astonishing accuracy.

Despite years of research, Croiset never really knew how his psychic power functioned. Once he described it as like seeing a fine powder which formed first into dots, then into lines. Out of these lines shapes and scenes would form, first in two dimensions, then three. Mostly he saw things in black and white, but curiously, if a corpse was involved, colour emerged.

Though his fame was established through his work as a psychic detective, the greater part of Croiset's life was taken up with healing. He declined payment for detection, saying that the only reward he wanted was for an account of each case to be kept in Professor Tenhaeff's records.

Croiset died on July 20, 1980, but the files at Utrecht University are a fitting memorial to a man who offered his psychic powers to help others.

CHAPTER EIGHT
Spiritual Healers

Perhaps the most dramatic advance in recent years
in the acceptance of paranormal powers has been in
the sphere of healing. Thousands now go to spiritual or
unorthodox healers, and claim to gain great benefits
and even cures.

Harry Edwards

Harry Edwards was considered by many to be the greatest spiritual healer this country has ever known. White-haired, stocky, dark-suited, he could have been taken for any city businessman except for one thing: his charisma was such that he drew thousands to watch him heal in public and thousands more were inspired to write letters to him.

He was, he claimed, guided by the spirits of Lord Lister, the founder of antiseptic surgery, and by Louis Pasteur, the great French scientist. His patients ranged from the very poor to members of the royal family, foreign rulers, cabinet ministers, army commanders, judges and bishops. Lady Baden-Powell, wife of the founder of the Boy Scout movement, was a regular visitor to his Spiritual Healing Sanctuary at Shere, deep in the Surrey countryside. So too was Princess Marie Louise, grand-daughter of Queen Victoria. Famous conductor Sir Adrian Boult received healing from him, and so did the ex-Queen of Spain.

With strong, workmanlike hands he seemed to achieve miracles by soothing away pain, remoulding twisted limbs, banishing disease and restoring sight and hearing. He did not always have to be in the same room. Sometimes he achieved what he called Absent Healing, when he was hundreds of miles away from his patient. Huge files exist bulging with letters confirming that his treatment had worked, yet he never had any medical or surgical training and was not instructed in any school of psychology.

His origins were quite ordinary. Harry Edwards was born in Crayford Street, Islington, in 1893, the eldest of nine children. His father was a compositor in the printing industry. His mother, the driving force of the family, who lived into her nineties to see him become famous, worked as a Court dressmaker for a firm which had premises at the back of Liberty's in Regent Street, London.

He was a young tearaway, a holy terror who was constantly being punished for some misdeed or other. The family moved house several times in South London, but his formative years were in Wood Green. He became a reformed character when he fell in love with a butcher's daughter at the age of twelve.

After leaving school at fourteen, he was apprenticed to a publishing house where his first job was as a floor sweeper at six shillings a week. He slowly climbed the ladder until he became a 'reader', checking printers' proofs for error. Discovering politics, he became an ardent Liberal, often standing on a soap box at Hyde Park Corner to support his cause. But he was not successful as a candidate and had to content himself with being an organizer.

During the First World War he served with the Royal Sussex Regiment. He started off in the ranks, but when his battalion embarked for service in India in 1915 he found himself promoted by degrees. After a crash course in engineering, including bridge-building (which he swore lasted no longer than sixty minutes), he was sent off to join the General Headquarters of the Mesopotamian Expeditionary Force in Baghdad.

One day he was sent for by General Marshall, who asked him if he would like a commission. Edwards thought this preferable to being a corporal and answered, 'Yes, sir'. After being 'commissioned in the field' he was sent to Tekrit, a walled Arab town not far from Baghdad. Here he found himself in charge of a wild bunch of nomadic Arabs with instructions to lay a railway track between Tekrit and Baghdad.

He was remarkably successful, and so impressed his superiors he was sent to the sun-baked hills of north-west Persia (now Iran) with the grand title 'Assistant Director of Labour, Persian Lines of Communication.' He ended up with the rank of Acting Major and the task of building roads and bridges strong enough to carry military equipment, in the most inhospitable terrain.

Strangely enough it was here, as a slender, fair-haired young officer, that Harry Edwards showed the first glimmer of his great gift for healing. Local labour was used, and that meant women and children as well as able-bodied men clamoured for jobs. Casualties were high, if not serious, among the unskilled workers, and the 'director', with little more than iodine, bandages and castor oil in his medical kit, found himself expected to cure everything. Strangely enough, he found even chronic conditions of illness among these rough hill people responded to his quiet touch. Soon everyone in the area had heard of the great 'Hakim'.

One day a local sheikh decided to bring his aged mother for treatment. The frail old lady had been placed in a sort of curtained box on the side of a horse and one look told Major Edwards that she was pitifully weak, in great pain and not far from death. He knew he could not ask the sheikh to take her away and let her die in peace — he would most likely have been killed for refusing his 'treatment'. On the other hand, he had not the remotest idea what was wrong with her, and had only the contents of his primitive medicine box to deal with the emergency. After examining her carefully, laying his hands on her body and praying for inspiration, he quickly prepared a potion from carbolic toothpowder. He gave it to her with trepidation and groaned inwardly as the satisfied sheikh took her away again with a large bottle of 'Hakim's' medicine. When the sheikh returned again a few days later accompanied by an escort of tribesmen yelling and firing off their rifles, Edwards thought he was about to meet his end. Instead the sheikh greeted him with joy, saying he had come to tell the great 'Hakim' that his mother was completely recovered, was free from pain and looking better than she had done for years. To show his gratitude he had brought gifts of carpets and gold pieces worth a fortune. Edwards had to refuse, but pressed to accept a gift of some kind mentioned he would like to have some fresh eggs for breakfast. Next day three hundred arrived!

Though the war ended in 1918 it was not until three years later that Acting Major Edwards arrived home. He married Phyllis White, a farmer's daughter from Long Bredy in Dorset, who had written to him all through the long years he had been abroad, and they moved into a house in Balham. Printing was the only trade he knew, so with high optimism he sank all his savings and his war gratuity into a print-works of his own. Everything went wrong. Though his married life was happy and he became the proud father of four children, his business lurched from one awful crisis to another. For the next twelve years he lived with the threat of closure and bailiffs at the door. He had, fortunately, the great gift of being able to lock up his troubles at the end of the day and lead a fulfilling life in other spheres.

He returned to politics, and gradually moved into public life. He was asked to stand for London County Council, worked for the League of Nations and after his printing business began at last to prosper, became chairman of Camberwell Peace Council.

His first contact with Spiritualism was at a church in Clements Road,

Ilford, Essex. He was by no means an easy convert. One of his hobbies was conjuring; he had a number of friends in the Magic Circle and he attended the Spiritualist Church in the first place to see whether he could work out what trickery was used to produce phenomena. To his surprise, the clairvoyant made a deep and lasting impression on him. When he attended another church at Cloudsdale Road in South London some time in 1934, he was told there were spirit guides who wished to co-operate with him and that he had undoubted powers of healing. He decided to test his views by trying to develop any psychic powers he might possess.

Through 'home circles' held in his own front room and at the houses of friends, he began to heal. Results were so good that he soon began to set aside several evenings a week specifically for that purpose. His first experience of healing someone who was miles away from him came with dramatic suddenness. He had been told by a medium that the next time he heard of someone desperately ill he must concentrate all his mind upon them. The opportunity came a few days later. While attending a home circle, someone told him about a friend of hers who was dying in Brompton Hospital from advanced tuberculosis with pleurisy and haemorrhages. He suggested they might try a healing experiment. Harry Edwards told what happened next in his *Thirty Years a Spiritual Healer*:

> We sat quietly in meditation, employing our thoughts for his recovery. As I did this, with my eyes closed, I became aware that I

Harry Edwards heals a crippled child

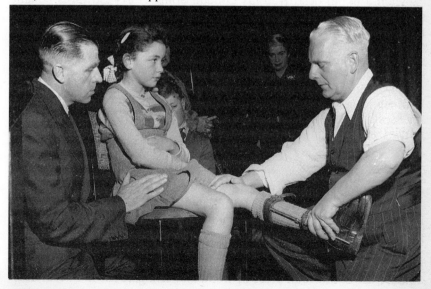

was looking down a long, hospital ward with my attention focused on a man in the last bed but one. I was conscious of all the surrounding detail and of the man himself. So strong was this picture that even over thirty years later I can revive it at will in all its vivid detail. When I checked the description of what I had 'seen' with a relative of the patient, it was found to be correct in every detail. It proved to be my first experience of 'astral travelling'.

A week later he received news that within twenty-four hours of his intercession the haemorrhages had ceased, all pleuritic pain vanished and the patient's temperature came down to almost normal. At the next check it was found that the blood and sputum were free from infection. The doctors were amazed. Within three weeks he was well enough to be sent to a convalescent home prior to discharge. Within months he was able to resume full employment, and subsequent inquiries established that the recovery had been maintained.

Harry Edwards, still regarding his gift with an open mind, was prepared to accept that this man's recovery could have been a remarkable coincidence, but when other incidents of a similar nature occurred he was convinced of his psychic power. Before long his work was known throughout South London and he had to set aside more and more time for healing. His fame spread through the war years. He considered himself 'simply as an instrument or a channel for a higher power', though he received many letters from patients who had never been in his presence saying they had seen a man in a white coat bending over them at the time of healing.

When a bomb destroyed his London home Harry Edwards bought a typical suburban semi-detached house at Ewell in Surrey and turned the front room into his first Spiritual Healing Sanctuary. In the early days he was in the habit of using many techniques suggested by other spiritualists, including trying to link thoughts with his patient and seeking a trance-like state for himself. As the years went by he found all these things unnecessary. His methods became increasingly simple but increasingly effective. He would talk quietly with the sick person, lay hands upon the affected part of the body and in his quiet, authoritative voice tell the sufferer that his or her ailment was under control. Absent healing, too, became simpler when he found that his practice of asking a distant patient to concentrate on his illness at a specific time was not necessary. Once he had set his healing power to work it seemed to function regardless of time or space.

So many people were now writing to him and asking to see him that he had to employ a full-time secretary. He began to realize he was going to have to devote the whole of his life to healing.

The front room at Ewell became far too small for his ministry, so he began looking for something more spacious. In 1946 he was told of a house set in fourteen acres of woodland and gardens at Shere, deep in the Surrey countryside near Guildford. Burrows Lea, built at the end of the last century, rambling, comfortable and peaceful, was the perfect place for Harry Edwards. He took the plunge and bought it for £8,000, leaving himself with £18 in the bank.

After two years he began to get in the region of 3,500 letters a week, and as the number rose to over 9,000 he had to take on extra staff. Olive and George Burton joined him to help with the patients. Those who were able to travel to Burrows Lea were treated in a quiet, wood-panelled room like a chapel with a cross on the wall and masses of beautiful flowers from Harry Edwards's own garden. He loved flowers and grew and picked them in profusion. He usually performed his healing in a white coat. His hands were always left uncluttered, and he wore neither rings nor a watch. He believed the first task of a healer was to calm and steady the mind, and the first impression his patients got was of kindness, quiet strength and authority.

One of the most remarkable healing stories about him is told by Ramus Branch in his biography of the healer. (With his wife, Joan, Branch served with Harry Edwards for several years and took on the work of the Sanctuary after his death.) During harvest one August, Edward's young niece, Vivien, was critically injured in a farm accident. She was sitting on a tractor when a bale of hay slipped forward and knocked her under the heavy wheels. She suffered appalling injuries, her body being crushed and literally twisted into the ground. The tractor had to be jacked up to release her. After she had been carried gently to the farmhouse the local doctor arrived, examined her, then phoned the hospital. He was heard to say that she would probably be dead on arrival. Vivien's mother, Harry Edwards' sister, was informed of the accident and immediately phoned to ask him for absent healing. Vivien was still alive when she reached hospital but her family was warned that she would probably die during the night. Her injuries were too terrible for her to survive. Harry Edwards concentrated with all his power on trying to save his young niece. She did not die that night, or the day after. To the amazement of the whole medical staff she began to recover. Within five weeks she was well enough for them to consider her discharge; by Christmas, she was home.

Though reticent about naming VIPs and royal personages who went to him for help, Harry Edwards was openly delighted that he could do something for Lady Baden-Powell. He had, after all, been one of the first Boy Scouts to join the movement. She first contacted him when, due to keep an important appointment, she found her knee had become so swollen and painful that she could hardly walk. By telephone he told her to proceed with her plans and he would give her absent healing. Lady Baden-Powell had to be more or less carried to the train, but during the journey she began to feel better. By the time she reached her destination the pain had gone and so had the swelling.

After that she often went to Shere to be 'pepped up', as she called it.

His public healing demonstrations, which started in a small way but ended with audiences of five or six thousand people at the Royal Albert Hall, became an important part of his work. He always conducted these sessions in his shirt-sleeves, and emphasized the 'spiritual' nature of any healing that people were about to witness. But his mischievous sense of humour sometimes broke through. When he had been accused by sections of the Church of conducting his meetings in an atmosphere of hysteria he turned to the audience, slowly rolled up his sleeves and said, 'I'm going to start now. By the way, don't let's have any hysteria. It'll be in the papers tomorrow!'

Advancing years seemed to make no difference to his power as a healer. Ramus Branch tells how one cold, foggy November night be and his wife — who had not yet joined Edwards at the Sanctuary — went over to Brentford, Middlesex, to see him conduct a demonstration. It took place in an unheated church, the yellow lighting casting an unreal glow over the packed audience. Harry Edwards asked if there was anyone present who was in constant pain. A hand shot up at the back of the church and he beckoned forward the sufferer.

Very slowly down the aisle came one of the most pathetic sights I have ever seen. It was a man of, I should think, about forty. He had tousled black hair and a beard and his clothes were like a bundle of rags around him for he seemed to be like a tramp . . . but it was the way he walked that stunned everyone to silence; he seemed to be half-crouching and was shuffling sideways, almost crab-like.

After a quick examination Harry Edwards declared that the major part of the man's internal pain arose as a result of severe restriction imposed upon the abdominal organs by the badly twisted and fixed state of the spine. All the time the healing was in progress the patient hardly said a word, but when it was over and he stood upright he seemed transformed into a new person. 'I can recall now the gasps of astonishment from the congregation as the man who had been barely able to walk before now literally marched back to his seat.'

But it was the sequel to this healing that Ramus Branch said he would never forget.

After the service my wife and I walked along to Kew Bridge to catch a bus home. The fog was even thicker than earlier and I asked her to wait for a moment or two whilst I went into a café to get a bar of chocolate. As I came out I was aware of a tall figure suddenly striding very rapidly through the swirling fog; so fast was he going that I had to step back quickly to avoid colliding with him. In that brief moment I could see it was the rough bearded man . . . as we both stood on the pavement gazing after him, we could hear him singing to himself as he vanished into the November fog.

In the last years of his life Harry Edwards visited South Africa and Southern Rhodesia (now Zimbabwe) and gave demonstrations of healing before vast audiences in both Johannesburg and Bulawayo. Back home at Burrows Lea he continued healing till the very end. On December 7, 1976, after a day on which he had signed batches of letters and made plans for the following day, he went to sleep in a chair, never to wake again.

Rose Gladden

Rose Gladden was only nineteen when she became fully aware that she was a psychic healer. She walked into a dry-cleaning shop in London and found the owner slumped over his counter. He was obviously in terrible pain. When she asked him what was wrong he managed to gasp out, 'I have an ulcer.' She felt a great desire to help him but did not know where to start. She has a clear memory of a voice saying 'Put your hand there.' But where? He had not even told her where the ulcer was. To her amazement she saw a tiny light, like a star, appear over his left shoulder. It floated down and came to rest on the right side of his stomach. She placed her hand there, and as she did so felt another hand cover hers and hold it steady. She seemed to be giving out tremendous heat and could not pull away. After a few seconds the man began to come round. Suddenly, he sat up. 'It's gone. The pain's gone,' he cried and rushed to tell the man next door about the incredible woman who had come to collect her cleaning.

Rose walked home knowing that it had been an important day in her life. She felt she knew now what she had come into the world to do. She had to become a healer.

Born in Edmonton, London, in 1919, she was only seven when she first realized she had a special gift of some kind. If she sat next to anyone at school suffering an ache or pain, she knew instinctively. Placing her hand on the cheek of a small friend with toothache, she would feel a warmth flow through her and into the hand she was using. The ache would, nine times out of ten, disappear.

This useful bit of schoolgirl one-upmanship did not make her life easy, far from it. She could not explain to people what happened, and also had to cope with occasions when she saw things other people did not see. During her twenties there was a difficult time when her experiences almost overwhelmed her. It was only when she met someone who recognized her as a natural psychic and taught her how to control and use her abilities that things fell into place.

Over the next forty-five years, until she slipped into semi-retirement to write her autobiography in 1985, Rose Gladden became one of the most dedicated and successful healers in Britain. An attractive woman she married twice, her second husband, Peter, playing an important part at the healing centre they set up at their home at Letchworth in Hertfordshire.

In the early days Rose Gladden saw everyone that turned up at her door. If one of her cases had attracted publicity and she had been featured in the morning papers, there would be a long queue before breakfast was over. After she had treated a ten-year-old Hitchin boy who had been confined to a wheelchair and considered inoperable by doctors, he appeared in a newspaper photograph playing football. For the next few days she was inundated with calls from anxious mothers all over the country asking if she could cure their children.

'It was like a conveyor belt,' her husband Peter said. 'Rose felt she could not do her best for people. We had to get organized, get things on a more professional footing. There are the occasional miracle-type cures which happen, but more often than not healing is a slow, gradual process.'

Mrs Gladden's home was overflowing with files of letters and reports on people who had found relief from their suffering and sometimes had experienced complete cures. Sometimes she received patients who were at the end of their tether, who had suffered so much for so long without getting relief from orthodox medicine that they were on the brink of suicide. She was often able to bring relief within minutes.

She is anxious to stress that by no means everyone experiences instant cure from healing of this kind. People should not expect miracles every time. 'The majority of those who experience improvement find that it is gradual, taking place over a period of weeks. It depends on the individual.' She believes that healing is done through the mind. 'Your hands guide the healing force and give comfort but it is the concentration of the mind that is doing the healing. You have to attune yourself to the patient and act as a channel for the healing energy.'

Rose Gladden has been a great success on both sides of the Atlantic. In America and Canada she has travelled thousands of miles, lecturing to medical specialists as well as to members of the public. At one meeting in Canada she discovered two women had travelled a thousand miles to see her.

She was asked by professors at several American universities to co-operate with them on tests. At the University of California she was wired up to a patient, a boy with a very serious nervous disorder, so that they could record what took place during the healing process. 'I am willing to submit to any test if it helps people to understand,' she says with deep sincerity.

Maxwell Cade, a psychologist who has carried out important pioneering work in meditation, relaxation and altered states of consciousness, also asked her to work with him. She helped him in the discovery of distinctive brainwave patterns in healers. The research demonstrated that on at least one level healers had a measurable effect on their patients, who after a few minutes picked up and imitated the same brainwave patterns. Rose Gladden was fascinated by this. It confirmed the theory she had had all along about the importance of being attuned to her patient.

As a natural psychic she claims to be able to see the 'aura', the protective circle of light and colour surrounding each human being. She reads the aura for ill health. One day she found she could also see silver spots and lines all over the surface of the body. It was not until some years later that she realized she was seeing the points and medians used in acupuncture. People would describe their symptoms to her but she often felt their trouble was not where they imagined it to be. She often saw the real trouble pinpointed by light. 'I'd put my hand in the light and the pain would go.'

Though she sees auras and things that other people do not — she once told a conference of nurses they must be sure to treat the dead with dignity for they often hung around their discarded frames for some time — Rose Gladden is a sensible, practical woman. Often after a healing session she will give the patient advice on how to avoid repetition of the trouble. 'But a lot of people expect you to do it all. You're the healer,' they'll say. 'You do it for me. But don't tell me to stop smoking or change my diet.'

She knows that many doctors simply shrug when her kind of healing is mentioned. But she does not see it as a substitute for medicine, only as an extension of orthodox treatment.

Matthew Manning

When sixth formers at Ashlyns School, Berkhamsted, in Hertfordshire, heard that they were to be lectured on the subject of healing by a well-known psychic they had no idea what kind of person to expect.

Probably the last thing they imagined was anyone like Matthew Manning. Young, slender, hair fashionably long, clothes fashionably casual, someone they could relate to without any difficulty.

He was breaking new ground when he accepted the invitation to speak from the headmaster of Ashlyns. As far as anyone knew it was the first time a psychic healer had ever taken a sixth-form class in a comprehensive school. He told them how by the age of eighteen he had experienced more psychic phenomena that most people hear about in a lifetime; how he had fled to the Himalayas to sort himself out after being treated as a psychic curiosity in the media; and how while he was there he realized he wanted to do something positive with his psychic power and returned to England to start work as a healer. His chief concern, he told them, was to try to convince people that unfaltering faith in the possibility of self-healing was one of the most exciting prospects for the future.

Matthew Manning's destiny was probably settled, according to some authorities, when he was still in the womb. His mother had an extremely severe electric shock three weeks before his birth. Many great psychics are thought to have been 'triggered off' by a traumatic physical experience.

He was born in August 17, 1955, and grew to be a normal, healthy, intelligent boy. The Manning family lived in an attractive modern house, open-plan, with floor-to-ceiling windows. There was nothing 'spooky' about it. On the morning of February 18, 1967, when Matthew was eleven years old, the poltergeist activity that came to be associated with him started. His father came downstairs early in the morning to find a favourite silver tankard lying on the carpet instead of being on the shelf where it was usually kept. No one in the house knew anything about it; Matthew, his sister Rosalind, eight, and his brother Andrew, six, all pleaded not guilty. It was treated as a joke until the following Wednesday when the same thing happened again. This time, it was noticed, other objects in the room had been moved. They began to suspect something freakish was happening.

The phenomena increased in power and activity. During one severe attack all the chairs in the dining and sitting rooms were jumbled together not once but twice. Suspicion that it was Matthew who was innocently responsible for the poltergeist activity increased when things started to move around him when he was in other houses.

In 1968 the Manning family moved into a beautiful old house in the village of Linton in Cambridgeshire which had been built in 1550 and extended some time between that date and 1730. There were a few 'odd happenings' they remembered later, but nothing too disturbing. Not at first. Suddenly in 1970 Matthew's bedroom became the focus of the most extraordinary activity. There were footsteps and raps, cupboard doors flew open, boots were hurled about, cushions took on a life of their own. By Easter 1971, all hell was let loose. The heavy cupboard in Matthew's room lurched away from the wall and moved towards him, his bed shook violently and started to rise from the floor. He spent the rest of the night in his parents' room on the floor in a sleeping bag and said he would not sleep in his own room again 'until something was done about it'. Next morning when the family went down to breakfast the house was in turmoil, as though a bomb had hit it. For the next few days they were subjected to the most violent poltergeist activity they had ever known, some of it purely mischievous, some quite frightening. One morning the bed in which Matthew's sister had slept was found with two of its feet hanging out of a first-floor window. On more than one occasion he saw the words 'Matthew beware' scribbled on the wall in child-like handwriting.

Now a boarder at a public school, Matthew began to feel he was only safe when he went back there after the holidays. But in the summer term of 1971 the disturbances finally followed him there. His father had already put the headmaster 'in the picture', but after what happened it was only with some difficulty that he was persuaded to keep Matthew at the school. There was genuine concern that the upheavals in the dormitory would endanger O-level studies. Heavy steel double-bunk beds moved of their own accord, glowing lights appeared on the walls, bookcases were upturned and broken glass, pebbles, cutlery and pieces of wood were hurled at windows. Fortunately for Matthew, the matron of his school possessed a certain amount of extrasensory perception and was sympathetic.

During a weekend at home Matthew had his first experience of 'hearing' a spirit voice, that of Henrietta Webbe, who had once lived in the house. Trying to project himself into the past, he fell into something like a trance and after a time heard a soft woman's voice near his head. He asked her questions he had prepared beforehand and on waking recorded their conversation immediately. About this time he also found himself writing automatically in a handwriting different from his own. As these psychic abilities increased, the poltergeist disturbances began to wane.

The encounter with Henrietta Webbe had sparked off his interest in the history of his home, Queen's House, and in the people who had once lived there. He spent several mornings searching the Linton Parish Registers for clues, and believes that was the catalyst that sparked off the strange relationship that now began between him and a gentleman called Robert Webbe, who had died in 1733.

In June 1971 Webbe communicated with Matthew Manning through automatic writing and was to continue to do so for several years. It soon became obvious that he thought the house still belonged to him and he tried to assert his authority over the household. Robert Webbe introduced himself in person one dark November night when Matthew's parents had briefly gone into the village and his sister was asleep in her bed. There were several raps on the door, but when Matthew opened it, no one was there. His heart began to beat heavily. He was, after all, only sixteen. Another tapping noise came from the top of the staircase. Matthew looked up and saw a figure standing there. At first he thought it was a burglar and wondered what he should do. Then he noticed the figure swaying slightly as if trying to support himself on the sticks he carried. A burglar with sticks? Suddenly, noticing his very odd clothes, Matthew realized he was looking at an apparition. 'Yet he appeared quite solid, solid enough for me to have mistaken him for a real human being had his clothes not given him away,' Matthew wrote of his encounter in his book *The Strangers*. This was Robert Webbe.

'I saw that he wore a green coloured frock coat which was embroidered around the edges with yellow thread. . . .' began Matthew's detailed description of the ghost.

'While I stood dumbfounded, he spoke in a perfectly ordinary human voice, without any trace of an accent. It sounded like the voice of a man tired after making an effort to walk with difficulty, almost as if he were out of breath. 'I must offer you my most humble apology for giving you so much fright, but I must walk for my blessed legs,' he said, apparently aware that he had frightened me.

Matthew politely asked him to wait while he fetched something, then tore into the kitchen to find pencil and paper. Then he stood on the bottom step and made a shaky sketch of his ghost. He noticed a very strong, spicy smell. Before the sketch was finished the apparition turned on his heels and disappeared somewhere between the landing and a bedroom.

When Matthew Manning was only seventeen he was approached by a publisher, and agreed to write an account of all his psychic experiences. *The Link* which dealt with the poltergeist manifestations, was eventually translated into fifteen languages. Later he wrote about the ghostly encounter with Robert Webbe in *The Strangers*.

His psychic powers became so strong that for two years he put himself at the disposal of various scientists in countries as far apart as Sweden and Japan, so that he could be tested under controlled conditions. He became very disillusioned about the science of parapsychology, and felt he was constantly being made to repeat experiments not because scientists did not believe him but because they did not believe the findings of their colleagues.

For a few years he was not very happy. He felt he had become a psychic curiosity exploited by the media. He felt he should be doing something more positive, that he should not be pushed around.

He left everything behind for a time, took a trip to India and made a pilgrimage to the Himalayas. Looking out over the great mountains as the sun rose, he said he felt a presence unlike anything he had known before. He had begun to realize that he had a capacity for healing, and decided when he went home he would devote his life to it. Since then he has treated hundreds of people from all walks of life and with a wide range of problems.

CHAPTER NINE

Visionaries and Stigmatics

They seem set apart from the rest of us by private experiences that can never be explained.

Versailles

Visiting the Palace of Versailles one August afternoon in 1901, two middle-aged English ladies walked down a grassy path in search of the Petit Trianon and found themselves in the eighteenth century. The account of their extraordinary adventure, which they recorded in meticulous detail, has become a classic of psychic literature.

Neither Miss Ann Moberly, daughter of the Bishop of Salisbury and head of an Oxford women's college, nor Miss Eleanor Jourdain, headmistress of a private school in Watford, were of a whimsical or over-imaginative nature. At the time of their visit they had not known each other long, having only recently been introduced, and their friendship was still at the slightly formal stage.

Miss Moberly had gone to Paris chiefly in order to be able to visit the great International Exhibition. Miss Jourdain had a small apartment in the French capital and was already on holiday there when her friend arrived. They agreed to explore the historical and architectural sites of interest in Paris together during the day and attend the Exhibition in the evenings.

Saturday August 10 turned out to be overcast and grey with a light summer breeze. After the great heat they had suffered all week they enjoyed the freshness and planned to spend the afternoon at Versailles visiting both the great Palace and its famous gardens.

By the time they had walked through the vast gilded salons and endless corridors it was almost time for tea. They made up their minds, however, before returning to the city, to visit the small, beautiful country house known as the Petit Trianon, built by Louis XV for his mistress, the Marquise de Pompadour, but for ever associated with a future Queen of France, the tragic Marie Antoinette. In its spacious grounds enhanced by decorative bridges, waterfalls, pavilions and scented groves, they also looked forward to seeing the 'toy village' where in simple farm cottages Marie Antoinette amused herself by pretending to be a milkmaid, shepherdess or peasant wife.

Setting out to walk, parasols and Baedeker in hand, they came to the head of a long lake and struck away down to the right through a woodland glade until they came to another stretch of water with an impressive building reflected in its surface, which they concluded rightly was the Grand Trianon, a château constructed for Louis XIV. They passed it on the left and came up to a broad green drive, perfectly deserted. If they had followed it, they would have reached the Petit Trianon directly, but instead they crossed it and went up the lane in front of them.

Miss Jourdain was a little way ahead when Miss Moberly caught sight of a woman shaking a white cloth out of the window of a cottage at the corner of the lane. She was surprised that her friend did not stop to ask the way. Only afterwards did she learn that Miss Jourdain had seen neither the woman nor the building.

At this point the two ladies were not aware of anything strange in their surroundings. They chatted about Oxford and mutual friends there, carrying on steadily up the lane then making a sharp turn right past a group of buildings. Now they had the choice of three grassy paths. They elected to follow the centre one, largely because they could see two men ahead and thought they would ask for directions. They presumed they were gardeners as they saw a wheelbarrow and a pointed spade close at hand, but they were dressed in long, greyish green coats with small, three-cornered hats and might easily have been officials of some kind. The men directed them straight ahead and they continued as before, deep in conversation.

At this point Miss Jourdain saw a detached, solidly built cottage with a woman and a girl standing in the doorway. She particularly noticed their unusual dress. Both wore white kerchiefs tucked into the bodice. The woman was passing a jug to the girl, who wore an ankle-length skirt and close white cap. Miss Moberly saw nothing.

From that moment both began to feel an odd sense of unreality, though not being on terms of intimate friendship as yet, neither liked to mention the fact to the other. Miss Moberly wrote later: 'We walked briskly forward, talking as before, but from the moment we left the lane an extraordinary depression came over me, which in spite of every effort to shake it off, steadily deepened until it became quite overpowering.' She did not know that Miss Jourdain was experiencing the same depression: 'I began to feel as if I were walking in my sleep; the heavy dreaminess was oppressive.'

They came to a grotto within which was a garden kiosk, like a small bandstand. Sitting by the side of it was a man wrapped in a heavy, dark cloak, a large hat shading his face. Suddenly he turned his head and looked at them. His face was pockmarked, repulsive, rough and dark, its expression odious. Miss Jourdain felt 'something uncanny and fear-inspiring'. The two ladies felt a moment of genuine alarm.

The place was so shut in that we could not see beyond it. Everything suddenly looked unnatural, therefore, unpleasant. Even the trees behind the kiosk seemed to have become flat and lifeless, *like a wood worked on tapestry*. There were no effects of light and shade, no wind stirred in the trees. It was all intensely still.

The sound of running footsteps on the path behind them came as a relief, but when they turned no one was there. Then they noticed another figure had appeared, this time a handsome fellow with black curly hair who was 'distinctly a gentleman'. He called out to them with great excitement, '*Mesdames, mesdames, il ne faut pas passer par là,*' then, waving his arms with animation, '*Par ici . . . cherchez la maison*', indicating that he wanted them to take the path to the right, not the left, for it would then bring them to the house. They went instantly to a little bridge on the right, then turned to thank him. To their amazement, he had disappeared. They heard running footsteps again, but saw no one.

Once over the bridge they were on high ground until they reached a meadow from which at last the front of the Petit Trianon itself could be seen. They walked towards a flight of steps leading up onto the terrace. At that moment Miss Moberly saw a lady sitting in the rough grass which grew right up to the house, apparently sketching. She turned and looked as they passed. Her face was not that of a young woman but it was strikingly pretty. Miss Moberly did not know why, but she did not find it attractive. She had puffed-out fair hair which fluffed around her forehead and supported a shady straw hat. Her dress, of a light summer material, was cut low in the bodice and trimmed with a fichu folded handkerchief-fashion across the shoulders. Miss Moberly felt as though she was walking in a dream and that the lady was part of it. She caught sight of her again as she stepped up onto the terrace. Miss Jourdain had not seen the figure at all.

They walked round to the west side of the terrace, looking for an entrance and feeling that the stillness and oppressiveness were becoming unbearable. Suddenly a door opened, a young man ran out, banging the door behind him, and ran rapidly towards the ladies, telling them they must not remain there. He offered to escort them towards the main entrance off the courtyard. His manner was jaunty, his smile slightly mocking and though he did not wear livery they gained the impression that he was a junior footman. He led them through a formal French garden, walled with trees, into the courtyard and they made their way to the entrance hall.

Suddenly everything seemed normal again. A guide arrived and they were invited to join a party of French tourists who also wanted to look over the house. Coming out they were able to hire a carriage to take them back to Versailles for tea. They noticed during the short drive that the wind was blowing and everything seemed natural again.

Neither Miss Moberly nor Miss Jourdain mentioned the Trianon visit again for a whole week, then as the former began to write a descriptive letter about her holiday in France the scenes of that day came back one by one. She dropped her pen and turned to her friend: 'Tell me, do you think the Petit Trianon is haunted?' Miss Jourdain answered without hesitation, 'Yes, I do.' It was only then they started to compare notes and realized they had not always seen the same things at the same time.

They returned to England and it was not until three months later, when Miss Jourdain paid a visit to her friend's college in Oxford, that they realized how important it was to record everything accurately as soon as possible. Already they had allowed too much time to elapse to satisfy those seriously interested in psychical research. They decided, very wisely, that each of them should set down her own experience independently of the other and sign it.

Miss Jourdain revisited the scene alone in the following January. She felt stunned as she discovered the whole place had changed, or seemed to have changed, and the route she and Miss Moberly had followed was almost untraceable. She asked friends in Paris whether they knew any story about the Petit Trianon being haunted. They told her there was a story that Marie Antoinette's ghost had been seen in the garden in a light summer hat and a pink dress. Some people from the village of Versailles had even gone so far as to say the whole ghostly court appeared on the anniversary of the sacking of the Tuileries on August 10, 1792, the day which led to Marie Antoinette's death on the guillotine.

The English schoolmistress hurried back to England to confer with her friend. For the first time they allowed themselves to ask the question that had haunted them for twelve whole months. Was it possible that on that August day in 1901 they had wandered into the past, seen the last day of the French Court, and that one of them had looked into the face of Marie Antoinette?

Both ladies returned to the Trianon in 1904. They retraced their steps with growing consternation. The gateway through which they had a glimpse of a broad green drive was derelict, the drive a tangle of weeds. There were no longer three clear paths for them to choose from; no cottage anywhere in the vicinity where Miss Jourdain had seen the woman and child with the jug. The little kiosk was not to be found, nor the bridge over the ravine which they had crossed when directed by their 'gentleman'. There were no steps leading to the front of the house, and the door through which the young man had rushed was invisible from where they stood because a wall intervened.

For the next ten years the two ladies devoted themselves to the task of trying to reconstruct the Petit Trianon as they saw it that day from documentary research. They delved into old records and documents, read contemporary accounts, tried to identify the people they had met.

So careful were they in checking and double-checking all the evidence that it was not until 1911 that anything was published, when the whole story appeared under the title *An Adventure*.

For a long time it was difficult to obtain detailed information of the arrangement of the Trianon gardens and outbuildings as they were in the 18th century. However, by sheer good fortune, in 1903 an old map was found hidden in the chimney of a house outside Paris. It had been drawn by Marie Antoinette's landscape gardener, Mique, about 1780. On examining the map closely it was possible to identify the vanished kiosk, the grotto and the cottage which Miss Jourdain saw but which had long disappeared.

Scrutiny of other original papers proved the existence of three distinct paths, a well-kept green drive and an artificial ravine which could only be crossed by a bridge.

Miss Moberly examined a portrait of Marie Antoinette by Wertmuller and came to the conclusion that it could have been her ghost she saw, though at the time she thought her to have been a tourist in extremely old-fashioned dress. Even the repulsive-looking man who sat by the kiosk was eventually identified. In 1789 there had been a Creole at the Court of Louis XVI, the Comte de Vaudreuil, who was feared because he looked so evil with his pock-marked dark complexion. He was in the habit of wearing a wide-brimmed hat to cover his face.

Miss Jourdain, who seemed to have the stronger psychic instinct, returned many times to Versailles during the years of research and sometimes felt there were people close to her she could not see.

The ladies remained friends for the rest of their lives. Miss Jourdain joined Miss Moberly at St Hugh's, Oxford, as her vice-principal and the two of them played a great part in pioneering, quietly and non-militantly, on behalf of women's emancipation. They were both loved and respected and considered to be of absolute integrity.

Their visions at Versailles have been taken up and dissected by many sceptics and critics, and dozens of explanations have been put forward. None of them hold water. Stories of death-bed confessions and the perpetration of a hoax have also been soundly disproved.

The two original accounts of 'The Adventure' were placed with the Bodleian Library in Oxford. The mystery of what happened on that August afternoon in 1901 remains to tantalize generations to come.

Joan of Arc

Voices, visions and dreams led the simple country girl who was Joan of Arc to be the saviour of France, the tragic martyr of Rouen and the saint who is still revered to this day.

Born of poor parents at Domrémy on the borders of Lorraine and Champagne on January 6, 1412, Joan was not what one would think of as the usual type of visionary. She was a strong, healthy country girl, with no sign of hysteria, who went about her daily work of helping in the house, spinning, sewing and looking after domestic animals with vigour and cheerfulness.

The voices started when she was only thirteen. She told her cruel inquisitors at a much later date, when her glory was over and she was facing death at the stake, that they often came to her when she was alone in the woods or sitting quietly in church. Sometimes even the steeple bells seemed to speak to her. They had one message. Her destiny was to go to the aid of France's rightful king and save her country. God would help her.

France was at this time in great danger. The conquering English were running amok over the fields and vineyards of their old enemy, capturing cities and castles and putting villages to the sword. At the same time the nation was being torn by civil strife, with the Burgundians and the Armagnacs at each other's throats.

The first voice she heard was that of the archangel St Michael, who, she said, returned to her again and again when she was alone in the fields. She also heard the gentler voices of the two patron saints of Lorraine, St Catherine and St Margaret, telling her to have courage.

In 1428 news came that the English were beseiging Orleans and if the city was captured it was more than likely that the whole of southern France would fall into the hands of the enemy. Joan's voices, as she told her inquisitors, became more insistent. St Michael told her she must go to the Dauphin (the future King Charles VII), win back the kingdom and see him crowned and consecrated. Joan protested, saying she was only a poor peasant girl and not a leader of men, but she heard the voice tell her clearly, 'Go to Messire de Baudricourt, Captain of Vaucouleurs, and he will take you to the Dauphin.'

Vaucouleurs was about ten miles from Domremy and it was difficult for Joan to get there. She was afraid what her father would do if he found out. He would never understand the voices, but she dared not disobey them. She was, however, shrewd and devised a plan by which she could get to Vaucouleurs. A relative of her mother's, an uncle by marriage, called Durand Laxart lived with his wife in a village not far from there. Prompted by Joan, he asked her parents to allow her to nurse his sick wife. They agreed, and Durand went to fetch her.

On their journey Joan reminded Durand of an old prophecy that France would be made desolate by a woman and restored by a maid from Lorraine. No one had any doubt that the woman who had ruined France was Queen Isabella, who had allied herself with the English, and Joan had no doubt that she was the maid from Lorraine destined to restore France to her former glory.

She told Durand to take her to Robert de Baudricourt without delay. There must have been authority in her voice, for her uncle did not hesitate. Baudricourt heard her story and said, 'Box her ears and send her home to her mother.' However, in due course he changed his mind. On February 12, 1429, she told him the French had been badly beaten by the English at the Battle of Herrings. They were hundreds of miles from the battlefield and the news was not received until two days later. Baudricourt took it as a sign that Joan was divinely inspired — some authorities believe she had a precognitive vision. He decided to send her to the Court at Chinon with two knights, Jean de Metz and Bertrand Poulengey, both of whom came to believe in her mission.

Joan got rid of her feminine clothes and dressed herself as a man with tunic, boots and leggings. She had her hair cut short and rode on an old horse bought for her by her uncle. Baudricourt gave her an old sword.

After reaching Chinon she had to wait for two days before being given permission to see the Dauphin. He received her at night in a hall lit by fifty torches. Three hundred nobles, magnificently dressed, watched as she entered. The Dauphin himself stood, in plain dress, apart from his throne, in order to test her. She knew him immediately and fell on her knees. He was so impressed that he took her aside and listened to what she had to say. Realizing he needed to be convinced that God had sent her to lead his armies, she demonstrated what could only have been a flash of psychic insight. She repeated to him his secret prayer that if indeed he was the rightful ruler of France, God would defend him, or at least allow him to escape in safety.

Joan of Arc at the stake on May 30, 1431

Though the Dauphin was completely won over, many of his council only half believed in her. But the situation was desperate, and, ready to try anything, they determined to send her with the troops about to be dispatched to the Duke of Orleans.

She now put on the accoutrements of a knight, being fitted out in a complete suit of white armour with a jerkin of scarlet and white. A great sword in a scabbard of red velvet hung at her side. The story of the sword became part of her legend.

It had once belonged to the great Charles Martel, who had stopped the Moslem invasion of France in the eighth century. For hundreds of years it had been hidden away, and few people knew where it was. Joan listened to her voices. They told her to ask for the ancient sword marked with five crosses which was buried in St Catherine's church at Fierbois. The clergy at Fierbois said they knew of no such sword. Joan told them that it was buried just behind the altar. Shovels were fetched, and the sword was found.

She rode from Chinon on a magnificent charger carrying a white banner fringed with silk and painted with fleurs-de-lys. At Blois she was given command of six thousand men collected for the battle to relieve Orleans. Appalled by the rabble she saw before her, she set to work to create a proper army. Camp followers and prostitutes fled, the foul oaths and blasphemies stopped. She ordered all soldiers to be regular in their attendance at Mass and to be clean and decent in their appearance. She filled them with the fire of patriotism, reminding them they were each and every one fighting, under God, for the glory of France.

Before setting out for Orleans she dictated (for she had never learned to write) a summons to the King of England, the Duke of Bedford, the Earl of Suffolk and two other English commanders, ordering them to surrender the keys of all the cities they had taken to the Maid who was sent by God to restore the royal blood of France.

Everywhere she rode, white banner streaming over her head, the French rallied to her and the English, suspecting she was of the devil, fled. After raising the seige of Orleans and gaining a great victory at Patay, Joan went to Rheims to see the Dauphin crowned in the Cathedral. Throughout the ceremony she stood by his side.

As soon as the coronation was over and Charles VII on the throne, Joan felt her mission was over. She asked permission to hang up her sword and return home. A foreboding of death came over her.

Many nobles were jealous of her success, the English wanted her dead at all costs. A treacherous and cowardly deal was arranged, and for a colossal sum the Burgundians handed her over to her enemies. The one man who could have saved her, the King of France, was too cowardly to come to her rescue. Brought before the Inquisition, mercilessly hounded by the brutal Bishop of Beauvais and abandoned by her voices, she was a tragic and pathetic figure. Initially she was indicted on seventy counts, many of them charges of witchcraft and sorcery, but by the time the trial was half over the count had been reduced to twelve and all references to witchcraft eliminated except one. After a trial that was both cruel and corrupt she was eventually condemned to death for her resistance to the Church. Almost her last words in prison to the Bishop of Beauvais were, 'Bishop, I die through you.' She realized that he, a Frenchman, was her worst enemy and had refused her every right.

Pronounced a relapsed heretic, Joan of Arc went to the stake at daybreak on May 30, 1431. An English soldier made a cross of two sticks and gave it to her as the fire was lit. A quarter of a century after her death, Joan was formerly exonerated and rehabilitated by the Church that had condemned her; in 1894 she was beatified and in 1920 declared a saint by the Pope. But from that day to this no one has been able to give an explanation for her voices and visions.

Bernadette

Bernadette Soubirous was a peasant girl of the greatest simplicity, belonging to a family that lived in abject poverty. She was poorly educated, asthmatic, hard-working and devout. Gathering firewood on the outskirts of the little town where she lived at the foot of the Pyrenees one cold February day in 1858, she looked up and saw the Virgin Mary.

Since then millions of people have made their pilgrimage to the place where she had her vision, and where the 'beautiful lady' appeared to her again and again. Lourdes has become a religious centre of the greatest importance to the Catholic faith, a focus of hopes and seemingly miraculous healing. Yet when Bernadette first spoke of what she had seen 130 years ago, she was beaten, accused of lying and regarded with suspicion by her parish priest.

No saint could have had a humbler beginning. Bernadette was born at Lourdes in 1844, the eldest child of an impoverished family. It was then a quiet place of mill streams, sheep and sun-baked rocks, the town itself a warren of narrow streets. Her father, François Soubirous, had been a miller but was sacked when he lost the sight of his right eye in an accident. By 1856 the family was in such dire straits they could not afford to pay rent and had to leave their simple house for a disused, vermin-ridden shack.

When cholera broke out in the Bigorre region of the Pyrenees where they lived, Bernadette was an early victim. Though she recovered she suffered from asthma for the rest of her life. For two years there was famine in Lourdes. Bernadette's father was arrested when he tried to steal for his family. It was decided that she should be sent away to stay with relatives in a mountain village where she would have food and a chance to regain her health tending sheep in the clear, pure air.

Above all things fourteen-year-old Bernadette wanted to learn her catechism and make her first communion. Her education had been neglected while she tried to earn money by working as a servant and as a waitress in a small café. She asked to be allowed to return to Lourdes and enrolled at the free school run by the Sisters of Charity.

Then came the February morning when she set out with her sisters to gather firewood. The girls crossed the River Gave by the old bridge leading out of the town, walked through an area of scrub, then came to the mill stream and a cliff face with a grotto. Two of the girls crossed the mill stream. Bernadette hesitated, then bent down to take off her stockings and shoes. She heard a noise like a gust of wind, looked up and saw a soft glow in the grotto. As her eyes became accustomed to the light a figure in white appeared with a soft, white veil falling each side of her face. Years later Bernadette wrote:

> I put my hand in my pocket, and I found my rosary there, I wanted to make the sign of the cross . . . I couldn't raise my hand to my forehead . . . The vision made the sign of the cross. Then I tried a second time and I could. As soon as I made the sign of the cross, the fearful shock I felt disappeared. I knelt down and I said my rosary in the presence of the beautiful lady. The vision fingered the beads of her own rosary, but she did not move her lips. When I finished my rosary, she signed for me to approach but I did not dare. Then she disappeared.

On the way home Bernadette told her sisters what she had seen, referring to the figure as 'Aquero', which meant 'that one' in local dialect. They had seen nothing. When the story of the vision was repeated to their mother she became frightened, thinking that her eldest daughter was beginning to 'see things', to hallucinate. She thrashed all three girls and forbade Bernadette to go to the grotto again.

At confession that Sunday Bernadette told the priest what had happened but he merely thought her fanciful. Her parents, however, relented and allowed her to go back, this time with a bottle of holy water. For the second time the vision in white appeared, a blue sash round her waist, a yellow rosary round her neck. Nothing could distract the peasant girl from what she saw, and eventually, almost in a trance state, she had to be carried back to her home.

For the first time a whisper of interest ran through the town. Some

Catholic pilgrims taking part in a candlelight procession at Lourdes

thought the girl was trying to create a sensation, others were impressed by her sincerity. Her mother was angry and upset. The identity of the vision had still not been established. Bernadette still called the lady in white 'Aquero', but there was a theory among some of the devout people of Lourdes that it could be the soul of a pious girl who had died the year before. But when Bernadette summoned up courage to speak next time she knelt in the grotto she was told it was not necessary for her to know who 'Aquero' was. Speaking for the first time, the vision in white asked her to go to the grotto every day for fifteen days, telling her, 'I do not promise to make you happy in this world, but in the next.'

Between February 18 and March 2, Bernadette saw her white lady thirteen times. She discovered a spring in the grotto, and rumour went round that those who drank from it would be cured of their ills. The story spread to other towns and villages, and soon thousands of people congregated along the river bank trying to catch a glimpse of the miracle that was happening in their midst.

Not everyone was impressed. The parish priest treated her with the deepest suspicion; the police commissioner implied she was making a nuisance of herself, warned her not to go to the grotto again and admitted he did not know what to make of her. She was interviewed by the town's Imperial prosecutor, the examining magistrate and the regional commandant of constabulary, who was extremely perturbed about the ever-growing crowds. They all conceded that whatever the truth, Bernadette Soubirous appeared to be sincere, sane and modest.

The crowds became so pressing that eventually she had to be escorted to the grotto by armed soldiers and wore a hooded cloak to cover her face. A deep hush fell as she knelt and raised her eyes to gaze on the mysterious figure no one else could see. The Church kept silent until Bernadette told Father Payramale, the parish priest, that her white lady had instructed her that people were to be allowed to approach the grotto in procession and that a chapel must be built there. His reaction was one of perplexed anger, and he demanded a miraculous sign before he would believe her.

Bernadette returned to school, thinking her visions had come to an end, but on the morning of March 25, the Feast of the Annunciation, she woke up with a strong desire to revisit the grotto. This time the white lady revealed that she was 'The Immaculate Conception' (the complicated doctrine of the immaculate conception of the mother of Jesus had been proclaimed in 1854). This time the Church listened. Payramale was convinced at last that she had seen genuine apparitions of the Virgin Mary.

Two weeks later Bernadette went to the grotto before dawn. She knelt with a long candle in her hands but seemed to be in such a trance that she did not notice when the flame burned down through her fingers. A doctor in the crowd examined her hands afterwards. There was not a mark on them.

From then on Lourdes and its grotto became the destination of pilgrims from all over the world. Sick people were already arriving in their thousands. Bernadette, unable to return to the simple life she had led, found sanctuary in the local hospice of the Sisters of Nevers. In 1866 she asked to join the order, and went as a novice to the mother house. She remained a nun until she died in 1879 at the age of thirty-five. She suffered greatly through several long illnesses and became increasingly reluctant to talk about her visions.

Bernadette of Lourdes was beatified in 1925 and canonized in 1933. Today it is estimated more than three million pilgrims a year make their way to her grotto. She would hardly recognize it.

Padre Pio Forgione

Padre Pio Forgione, a gentle Italian priest who died in 1968, was the most celebrated stigmatic since St Francis displayed the wounds of Christ in the thirteenth century. For fifty years he suffered agony from the terrible bleeding holes in his hands and in his left side. But he had no time for those who wanted to make him a saint.

For most of his life the humble Capuchin friar lived a life of strict devotion in the Italian monastery of San Giovanni Rotondo at Foggia. Far from exploiting his stigmata, he tried to avoid publicity and often covered his hands in public. But the world clamoured to see him.

With his grizzled beard and blunt features, Padre Pio looked like a peasant. He was born in the village of Pietrelcina near Benevento in 1889. His father was a poor farmer, and the Forgione family lived a frugal life, close to the soil. Padre Pio knew his vocation from an early age and at the age of seventeen entered a Capuchin monastery as a novice. During his youth and early priesthood he had a delicate constitution which was seriously affected by rigorous fasts and harsh discipline. He developed tuberculosis, began to see apparitions and was subject to 'diabolical attacks' which were similar to poltergeist outbreaks in which the sparse furniture in his cell moved of its own accord, his few possessions were scattered and his bedclothes thrown to the floor.

In 1915, when he was twenty-eight, he emerged from a long period of meditation with a queer stinging sensation in his hands. No one knew what to make of it, and it was soon forgotten. It was not until three years later that the significance of the sensation was realized.

On September 20, 1918, he was praying alone in the choir of the church at Foggia when, without warning of any onset of pain or illness, he gave a piercing cry and fell unconscious. His brother monks came running from other parts of the church to find him bleeding profusely from hands, feet and side. He showed, in other words, every sign of the stigmata, the five wounds suffered by Christ on the Cross.

Padre Pio begged those who had found him to keep his condition a secret, but word spread quickly of what had happened. From then on he was seldom free from pain and could move only with the greatest difficulty. The Provincial Superior who examined the wounds shortly after their appearance said that he would swear solemnly that he had seen clear through the holes well enough to have read print held on the other side. Sometimes as he lifted the Host during Mass he would pass into a state of ecstasy. A cupful of blood would flow from his wounds every day.

The faithful with Italy's semi-saint Padre Pio

It is interesting to note that genuine stigmata appear to have different characteristics from ordinary pathological wounds. The blood that flowed from Padre Pio's hands was clean, arterial blood, free from the discharges of disease, and there was no festering. Doctors of all denominations examined his stigmata many times over the years, but none could give a satisfactory explanation for his injuries. They dismissed the idea that the wounds could have arisen from any physical cause. Along with theologians they observed that most stigmatics are intensely devout people given to brooding deeply on the sufferings of Christ. The twentieth-century explanation is that an element of auto-suggestion is involved, but nothing has been proved.

Whatever the cause in Padre Pio's case, he carried on his duties with humility in spite of the open adulation of the peasants and the growing cult that surrounded him. Thousands began to descend on the church in Foggia, hoping to catch a glimpse of him. Money was sent to the monastery from people in all walks of life. The Vatican twice suspended him from his duties. The attitude of Rome from the beginning had been one of caution, and Padre Pio was aware that he was under constant surveillance by the religious authorities. When the money began to flow in his fame became something of an embarrassment, for he had taken a vow of poverty. Eventually he was absolved from his vows in this respect provided all the money sent to him was willed to the Church for charitable use.

In 1956 a hospital which cost in the region of £1 million was built at Foggia and completely paid for out of donations sent by people from all over the world who had come to see Padre Pio as a saintly figure. Even his home village of Pietrelcina began to prosper as crowds flocked to see the place where he had been born and brought up.

Apart from his fame as a stigmatic, Padre Pio had shown other signs that made him different from his fellow monks. He was credited with healing and other miracles and especially with clairvoyance.

Three men visiting the church on January 20 1936, were approached by Padre Pio, who asked them to pray with him for a soul about to meet his God. They knelt with him and were then told by the priest that they had been praying for George V of England. He had died while they were on their knees.

Perhaps the most extraordinary story concerning Padre Pio's faculty for the psychic is that concerning a certain Monsignor Damiani of Salto in Uruguay. The South American gentleman had met Padre Pio while on a visit to Italy, and was so impressed he declared he wanted to die in the priest's presence. Padre Pio said to him kindly, 'You will die in your own country — but you will have no need to fear.'

Damiani returned to Uruguay. Years passed and in the summer of 1942 he fell ill. The Archbishop of Montevideo was awakened in the early hours of the morning by a Capuchin monk who urged him to go immediately to Monsignor Damiani's bedside. When he arrived Damiani was already dead but on the bed was a slip of paper on which was written three words: 'Padre Pio Came.' Several years later the Archbishop met Padre Pio and recognized him as the Capuchin monk who had come to him.

Padre Pio died on September 28, 1968.

Theresa Neumann

Bavarian peasant girl Theresa Neumann was said to suffer Christ's Passion every Lent for the last thirty-two years of her life. Great weals appeared on her back from the scourging, bleeding punctures marked her forehead where it had been pierced by the crown of thorns and her hands, feet and side gushed blood as though they had been torn by nails and a sword.

Few people were allowed near her. She spent most of her life in bed wrapped in white linen and seldom gave any sign of curiosity about the outside world.

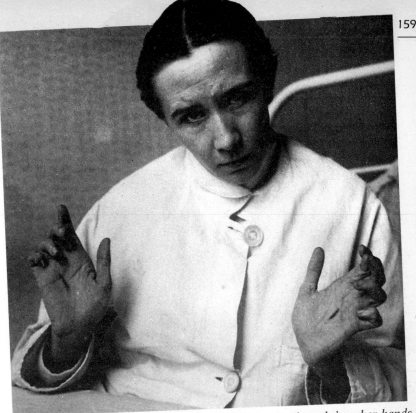

Theresa Neumann showing 'nail marks' on her hands

Born in 1898 in the village of Konnersreuth, Bavaria, she came from a very poor family but in her youth seemed no different from any other girl of her age. She went to work as a domestic on local farms, then suddenly succumbed to a series of mysterious illnesses which no doctor could explain.

During Lent 1926, when she was twenty-eight, she had an overwhelming vision of the Passion which cured her of her various afflictions but left her bearing the marks of the stigmata. Every Friday for the next thirty-two years she wept blood or bled from the wounds, but at Lent she went through the whole terrible ordeal of the Passion over again, writhing in agony, gushing blood from every wound. Sometimes she lost as much as a pint of blood and eight pounds in weight during her vision.

She was watched closely by the Bishop of Ratisbon, who wanted to protect her from the pilgrims, curiosity-seekers and miracle-hunters who poured into the village of Konnersreuth once her condition was known. Doctors were allowed to examine her thoroughly, taking advantage of her trances and periods of unconsciousness. Many said that her wounds bore a strong resemblance to those of St Francis,

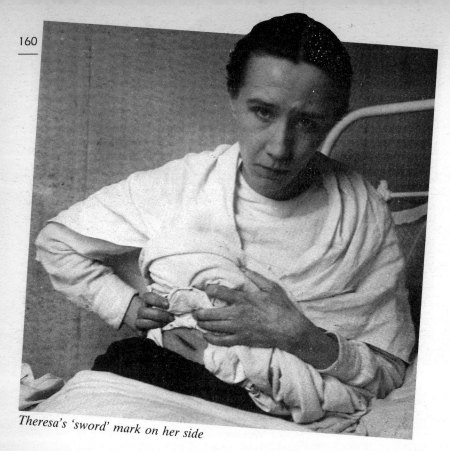

Theresa's 'sword' mark on her side

especially those on the hands which gave the impression of a forged iron nail piercing and protruding from them. The nail head was described as rectangular, admirably regular, its edges being delicately adorned with zigzag borders. The wounds remained dry until dawn broke each Friday, then the figure in white lying in bed would begin to stream with blood.

Theresa was said to be clairvoyant and to speak in Aramaic, Christ's own language, when in a trance. Another extraordinary aspect of her story is that no food or liquid, except the communion wafer and wine, had been seen to pass her lips for thirty-five years. Her total fast started in the twenties and she was subject to long periods of medical scrutiny. Doctors once kept her under strict surveillance for several weeks, night and day, but in the end testified that to the best of their knowledge nothing had passed her lips but the wafer and wine.

She was said to have remained in reasonable health, though photographs of her show a waxen, ghost-like image. Doctors noted that her excreta, which had progressively diminished since 1926, ceased altogether after 1930 and her intestinal tract simply withered away. She continued to have ecstasies and visions up to her death in 1962.